The Trillion Dollar
WAR

The Trillion Dollar WAR

The U.S. Effort to Rebuild Afghanistan, 1999–2021

ABID AMIRI

MARINE CORPS UNIVERSITY PRESS
Quantico, Virginia
2021

LIBRARY OF CONGRESS
CATALOGING-IN-PUBLICATION DATA

Names: Amiri, Abid, 1989– author. | Marine Corps University (U.S.). Press, issuing body.

Title: The trillion dollar war : the U.S. effort to rebuild Afghanistan, 1999–2021 / by Abid Amiri.

Other titles: U.S. effort to rebuild Afghanistan, 1999-2021

Description: Quantico, Virginia : Marine Corps University Press, 2021. | Includes bibliographical references and index. | Summary: "The Trillion Dollar War is the culmination of an Afghan's personal life story weaved into academic understanding and coupled with professional experience in the field of development. It is written for Afghans, Afghan policymakers, and those in the West and broader international community who truly wish to see Afghanistan progress after more than 20 years of war. This title offers a perspective on how the United States and Afghanistan got where they are and proposes ways to find the economic growth that has until now remained elusive"— Provided by publisher.

Identifiers: LCCN 2021046110 (print) | LCCN 2021046111 (ebook) | ISBN 9781737040569 (paperback) | ISBN 9781737040576 (Adobe pdf)

Subjects: LCSH: Marshall Plan. | Economic development—Afghanistan. | Economic assistance, American—Afghanistan. | Nation-building—Afghanistan. | Nation-building—United States. | Waste in government spending—United States. | Corruption—Afghanistan. | Afghan War, 2001–

Classification: LCC HC420.E44 (print) | LCC HC420.E44 (ebook) | DDC 330.9581—dc23/eng/20211103 | SUDOC D 214.513:AF 3/7

LC record available at https://lccn.loc.gov/2021046110

LC ebook record available at https://lccn.loc.gov/2021046111

DISCLAIMER

The production of this book and other MCUP products is graciously supported by the Marine Corps University Foundation.

Published by
Marine Corps University Press
2044 Broadway Street
Quantico, VA 22134

1st Printing, 2021
ISBN: 978-1-7370405-6-9

THIS VOLUME IS FREELY AVAILABLE AT WWW.USMCU.EDU/MCUPRESS

To my father Mohammad Rahim Amiri,
to my wife Huma, and to my children, Husna and Atif.

CONTENTS

ILLUSTRATIONS

TABLE

FOREWORD

It has always seemed problematic that most of the public debate about the war in Afghanistan and the economic development in that country has been conducted by non-Afghans. From academic literature to news articles, the Afghanistan discussion has been occupied by those in Washington, London, or Paris during the last two decades. The simple fact that *The Trillion Dollar War* is the work of an Afghan is the least of the reasons why you should read it. But it is a good reason nonetheless.

Born in Afghanistan and educated in the West, Abid Amiri brings to this subject a rare combination of academic expertise and real-life experience. His background in economics took him from the Embassy of Afghanistan in Washington, DC, to George Washington University, where he obtained his master's degree in international development, and then on to working under my supervision at the Ministry of Finance of Afghanistan. It is an impressive résumé. I have known him for more than 10 years, and he has always impressed me as someone who wants to do good for his people and humanity at large, beginning with this impressive work.

Although he is not the first writer to criticize development aid programs in Afghanistan, never has the case for a unique approach to aid distribution been made with such rigor and conviction. Why, asks Amiri, does Afghanistan flounder in a seemingly never-ending cycle of poverty, corruption, and aid dependency, despite the fact that approximately $1 trillion (USD) has poured into the country since 2001? His answer is simple: the way that the aid money has been disbursed is precisely the problem.

The author offers a study of the 1948 Marshall Plan (known more formally as the European Recovery Plan) experiment in Europe following the end of World War II and draws conclusions from it to apply to Afghanistan today. After the war, Europe was as devastated as Afghanistan was in the early 2000s. According to Amiri, the European Recovery Plan, which cost only $15 billion over four years, triggered a chain of events leading to massive economic growth across the continent.[1] However, Afghanistan during the past 20 years has exhibited minimal economic growth, while the influx of aid has been significantly higher.

Why is this? Amiri recounts some of the more egregious examples of aid-fueled corruption. In November 2012, the U.S. federal government hit a large American construction company with the highest fine in a wartime contracting case after a whistleblower revealed that the company had overbilled the government and paid insurgents to protect the project.[2] According to an Integrity Watch Afghanistan survey report, more than 4.6 million Afghans paid some sort of bribe in 2018. The total bribe paid that year amounted to more

---

[1] Also known as the European Recovery Program, the Marshall Plan provided aid to Western Europe following the devastation of World War II. It provided more than $15 billion to help finance rebuilding efforts. "Marshall Plan, 1948," Office of the Historian, Foreign Service Institute, Department of State, accessed 7 July 2021.

[2] "Whistleblower Exposed Fraud by the Louis Berger Group; $69.3 Million Settlement Sets Record for Afghanistan and Iraq Contractor Fraud Case," Cision PR Newswire, 5 November 2010.

than $1.65 billion, which is about 9 percent of the total gross domestic product (GDP) of Afghanistan.[3] As the country's former minister of finance, it was my responsibility to fight the corruption inside and outside the government.

Amiri offers a simple alternative for the way aid ought to be distributed in Afghanistan: help Afghanistan help itself. In his mind, "Afghanistan needs an economic recovery program and not a humanitarian relief effort. The current ad hoc and humanitarian relief-oriented assistance has made little impact on the economy of Afghanistan." He suggests that a massive intervention like the Marshall Plan is required to jumpstart the Afghan economy. In addition, the funds must be invested heavily in areas directly or indirectly associated with the private sector. Finally, the government of Afghanistan must make economic policy reforms to support its domestic private sector.

Most importantly, Amiri outlines the fundamental importance of a self-reliance policy (with zero aid) to be implemented in Afghanistan. Instead of relying on ad hoc foreign aid, self-reliance, including how to use its own resources and to lend from financial institutions, should be the ultimate goal.[4]

Amiri prescribes strong medicine for the war-ravaged country. But those who read *The Trillion Dollar War* will have no doubt that his primary motivation is to reduce hardship for ordinary Afghans. This book

---

[3] The data for 2018 and 2020 are available in *National Corruption Survey* (Kabul: Integrity Watch Afghanistan, 2018 and 2020).

[4] "Afghanistan—Journey to Self-Reliance: FY 2021 Country Roadmap," USAID.gov, accessed 8 July 2021.

represents an Afghan view of Afghanistan's economic problems for the policymakers in Washington, London, Paris, and Kabul.

Eklil A. Hakimi
Former Minister of Finance of Afghanistan
Former Ambassador of Afghanistan to the United States

PREFACE

I was born in Kabul in 1989, the year the Soviet Union withdrew all its troops from Afghanistan. It was the end of one ferocious era and the beginning of a new dark episode for Afghanistan. By 1991, the *mujahideen* took over Kabul and there was considerable violence throughout the city.[5] One day, some of these armed militants broke into my family's house in Kabul. They stole some of our property and threatened to shoot my father. Because of this violence and the deteriorating security situation in Kabul, the capital city, my family decided to move out of Afghanistan in 1992. We became immigrants in Peshawar, Pakistan. My father worked at a store, and my mother stayed home with us. I helped my father in the store and attended school in Peshawar. It was a very difficult life. We struggled to survive in exile. My early life's journey is no different than millions of other Afghans who went through similar hardships or faced even more challenges.

Growing up as a refugee in Pakistan, my textbooks, notebooks, and pens were all donated by the U.S. Agency for International Development (USAID), the United Nations Children's Emergency Fund (UNICEF), and other development agencies. I remember getting so

---

[5] The term *mujahideen* refers to members of guerrilla groups operating in Afghanistan during the Soviet-Afghan War (1979–92) that opposed the invading Soviet forces and eventually toppled the Afghan Communist government.

excited when international aid donors would come in to give us school supplies. The USAID-branded cooking oil containers were ubiquitous in every immigrant's house. The United Nations (UN) provided food ration containers that could be seen throughout the refugee camps.

In 2001, the United States and its allies removed the Taliban regime from Afghanistan. After living almost nine years as immigrants, my family decided to return to Kabul with high hopes. We returned from exile to try and pick up our lives again in our home country. My father returned to his job at Da Afghanistan Bank. My brothers, sisters, and I attended school in Kabul. We all felt at home after nine years of a life in exile in Pakistan. In 2003, when I was in the 10th grade, I applied to participate in an exchange program for high school students to live and attend school for one year in the United States. I applied for the program along with more than 3,000 other students from across Afghanistan. I was accepted and started my exchange student journey in the summer of 2004.

The year that I spent in the United States as an exchange student was full of unique experiences. I learned a lot and even attended my junior prom. I was involved in different activities within the high school. I completed more than 100 hours of volunteer work in the community and was awarded the President's Volunteer Service Award from the White House, which was signed by President George W. Bush. I also had the opportunity to meet high-ranking staff in the U.S. Department of State, including Zalmay M. Khalilzad, who served as the U.S. ambassador to Afghanistan and later to the United Nations, and the governor of New York, George E. Pataki. I also met several U.S. senators when I visited Capitol Hill in Washington, DC.

After completing the exchange program, I returned to Kabul in 2005. The experience of living in an economically advanced country like the United States changed my perspective on many fronts. The long stretches of paved roads and highways, the level of comfort in all walks of life, running hot and cold water, 24-hour electricity, and broadband internet—everything that we did not have in Afghanistan—was taken for granted by the American population. It made me question why this massive divergence in these ways of life existed. Why was it that Afghans could not also improve their standard of living so that a student does not need to get so excited for a donor aid agency to provide their school supplies or so that a teenager does not need to perform hard labor to support their family?

This curiosity led me to study at St. Lawrence University in New York in 2007 on a full scholarship. I spent my formative years on campus, even during summers, conducting research about employment in Afghanistan, the Global War on Terrorism, etc. As a result of this research, I decided to study economics and global studies. Soon after graduation, I moved to Washington, where I spent a year working for a nonprofit before joining the Elliott School of International Affairs at the George Washington University. There, I studied international development to further strengthen my understanding of this field. At the same time, I worked at the Embassy of Afghanistan in Washington as an economist, where I helped coordinate events between the Afghan government and major international organizations involved in Afghanistan, such as the World Bank, the International Monetary Fund (IMF), and USAID. This experience gave me greater access to the world of development. In 2015, soon after completing my graduate education, I decided to return to Afghanistan and work at the Ministry of Finance.

The Ministry of Finance allowed me to find answers to the question, "Why can't Afghans also improve their standard of living?" My work experience gave me the opportunity to support one of the major international donor conferences for Afghanistan: the Brussels Conference on Afghanistan in 2016. It also allowed me to learn more about what is working and what is broken in the economic system of the country.

This book is the culmination of my personal life story weaved into academic understanding and coupled with professional experience in the field of development. It is written for Afghans, Afghan policymakers, and those in the West and the broader international community who truly wish to see Afghanistan progress. In what follows, I offer my perspective on how we got where we are and propose ways to find the economic growth that has until now remained elusive.

Today, I am able to write this book in large part thanks to the help of development organizations that provided me with notebooks, pens, and pencils. Otherwise, like many of my friends in the refugee camps who could not afford their books, dropped out of school, and later joined the ranks of the Taliban, I would have been a victim of the war too. The main reason I am so passionate about getting development aid right is that development aid is so very personal to me, as I have come out of the conflict zone successfully due to the help I received from aid agencies.

ACKNOWLEDGMENTS

We can all admit that 2020 was one of the most challenging and stressful years in recent memory, with a devastating global pandemic followed by a complete lockdown in most countries. However, in the midst of all the chaos, I found a great deal of comfort in writing this book. It has been a perplexing, exhilarating, wonderful, and exasperating journey. None of this would have been possible without the support of my wife, Huma Amiri, who listened to my book ideas, gave me feedback, and, most importantly, took care of our two children, Husna (age five) and Atif (age two), so I could focus on my writing.

Douglas Ferris, someone I dearly admire—my "American dad," as I call him—sponsored me as an exchange student and helped me go to a community college prior to introducing me to his alma mater, St. Lawrence University, where I received my bachelor's degree. He was instrumental in shaping who I am today. In addition, he helped me edit the content of *The Trillion Dollar War* and provided valuable feedback.

I also owe a great debt of gratitude to Former Minister Eklil Hakimi, who played a significant role in my professional life. He put a great deal of trust in a young man when he asked me to join him at the Embassy of Afghanistan, where he served as ambassador of Afghanistan to the United States. Later, he supervised me during my tenure at the Ministry of Finance and mentored me through challenging times.

Finally, I wish to thank my late father, Mohammad Rahim Amiri, for his unwavering support and belief in me every step of the way. He instilled a sense of nobility in me through his acts of kindness to others, which is what I am trying to achieve by writing this book.

SELECTED ABBREVIATIONS
AND ACRONYMS

ACJC	Anti-Corruption Justice Center
ADB	Asian Development Bank
AITF	Afghanistan Infrastructure Trust Fund
ANA	Afghan National Army
ANDS	*Afghanistan National Development Strategy*
ANDSF	Afghan National Defense and Security Forces
ANP	Afghan National Police
ANPDF	*Afghanistan National Peace and Development Framework*
ANSF	Afghan National Security Forces
ARTF	Afghanistan Reconstruction Trust Fund
BBC	British Broadcasting Corporation
CAREC	Central Asia Regional Economic Cooperation Program
CASA-1000	Central Asia-South Asia power project
CNN	Cable News Network
COIN	counterinsurgency
CSO	Central Statistics Office
ECA	Economic Cooperation Administration
EFT	electronic funds transfer
ERP	European Recovery Plan (a.k.a. Marshall Plan)
GDI	Gender Development Index
GDP	gross domestic product
GWOT	Global War on Terrorism
HDI	Human Development Index
IDLG	Independent Directorate of Local Governance
IEC	Independent Election Commission of Afghanistan
IED	improvised explosive device
IMF	International Monetary Fund
INL	Bureau of International Narcotics Control and Law Enforcement Affairs
ISAF	International Security Assistance Force
ISIS	Islamic State of Iraq and Syria
ISIS–K	Islamic State of Iraq and the Levant–Khorasan Province

ISP	individual salary payment
JICA	Japan International Cooperation Agency
LBG	Louis Berger Group
LOTFA	Law and Order Trust Fund for Afghanistan
NATO	North Atlantic Treaty Organization
NIP	*National Infrastructure Plan, 2017–2021*
NPP	National Priority Programs
OEF	Operation Enduring Freedom
SIGAR	Special Inspector General for Afghanistan Reconstruction
SMAF	*Self-Reliance through Mutual Accountability Framework*
TAP-500	Turkmenistan-Afghanistan-Pakistan Power Interconnection Project
TAPI	Turkmenistan-Afghanistan-Pakistan-India Pipeline
TMAF	*Tokyo Mutual Accountability Framework*
UN	United Nations
UNAMA	United Nations Assistance Mission in Afghanistan
UNDP	United Nations Development Programme
UNHCR	United Nations High Commissioner for Refugees
UNICEF	United Nations Children's Emergency Fund
UNOCHA	United Nations Office for the Coordination of Humanitarian Affairs
USAGM	United States Agency for Global Media
USAID	United States Agency for International Development
VMI	Virginia Military Institute
WWII	World War II
YES	Youth Exchange and Study Program

The Trillion Dollar
WAR

INTRODUCTION

According to a 2018 Gallup poll, 6 out of 10 Afghans reported that they struggled to afford food in the past year.[1] Two-thirds of respondents said that it was extremely difficult to get by on their household income. Former president Ashraf Ghani called the poverty rate of Afghanistan "shameful" after Afghanistan's Central Statistics Office (CSO) reported that more than 50 percent of the population was living below the poverty line.[2] According to a joint ICON International and CSO study, the share of people living in poverty has climbed in recent years, rising from 34 percent in 2007 to 55 percent in 2018.[3] Unemployment set a new record in 2018, with nearly one-third of Afghanistan's workforce jobless, and the numbers among the relatively few women in the workforce hit 67 percent—the highest ever recorded (figure 1).[4]

Corruption in Afghan institutions is a widespread and growing problem. In 2018, Transparency International ranked Afghanistan among the 10 most corrupt

[1] Justin McCarthy, "Inside Afghanistan: Record Numbers Struggle to Afford Basics," Gallup World Poll, 26 August 2019.

[2] Kathy Gannon, "Afghan Refugees Tell UN: 'We Need Peace, Land to Go Home'," ABC News, 17 February 2020.

[3] *Afghanistan Living Conditions Study, 2016–17* (Kabul: Central Statistics Organization [CSO] of the Government of the Islamic Republic of Afghanistan and ICON International, 2016).

[4] Kristjan Archer, "Inside Afghanistan: Job Market Outlook Bleakest on Record," Gallup World Poll, 9 September 2019.

Figure 1. Unemployment in Afghanistan, 2010–18

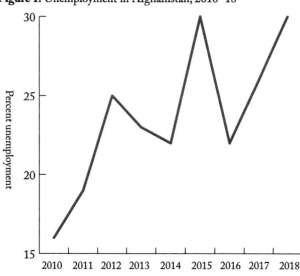

Source: Gallup World Poll, 2019.

countries in the world.[5] Various other anticorruption watchdog groups frequently call attention to corruption as an endemic problem in Afghan institutions. Government officials collect bribes in customs ports, service delivery, and health and medical services, which results in lower national revenue and destroys public trust in the government. Integrity Watch Afghanistan reported in 2016 that Afghans paid approximately $3 billion

[5] "Afghanistan," Transparency.org, accessed 28 January 2021. This list also included Somalia, South Sudan, Syria, Yemen, North Korea, Sudan, Equatorial Guinea, Guinea Bissau, and Libya.

(USD) in bribes in a single year, which is a 50-percent increase from two years prior.[6]

Afghanistan is ranked 169th out of 189 countries on the Gender Development Index (GDI), which measures gender disparity, or the ratio of female to male Human Development Index (HDI). Women in Afghanistan still face significant inequities in the areas of health (measured by female and male life expectancy at birth), education (measured by female and male expected years of schooling), and access to economic resources (measured by female and male income per capita).[7] On average, about 1,600 women die in childbirth out of every 100,000 live births in Afghanistan, while in remote areas of the country that number rises to 6,500. In more prosperous countries such as the United States and those in Europe, 9 maternal deaths occur for every 100,000 deliveries.[8] According to the most recent UNICEF report, 60 percent of Afghan girls are not in school, and one-third of girls marry before reaching the age of 18.[9]

---

[6] Ayaz Gul, "Survey: Afghans Pay $3 Billion in Bribes Annually," Voice of America News, 8 December 2018.

[7] The Gender Development Index measures the gender gap in human development achievements by accounting for disparities between women and men based on a long and healthy life, knowledge, and a decent standard of living. The ratio is calculated as female HDI to male HDI. A value equal to 1 indicates development equality between genders, while values further from 1 have less development equality between genders. "Gender Development Index (GDI)," Human Development Reports, United Nations Development Programme, accessed 22 May 2021.

[8] Tan Ee Lyn, "Death in Childbirth: A Health Scourge for Afghanistan," Reuters, 29 April 2008.

[9] *Afghanistan Annual Report, 2017* (New York: UNICEF, 2017).

According to a recent Gallup poll, Afghans' trust in their democratic institutions has continued to erode. Confidence in the national government remains at 36 percent.[10] One out of every four Afghans did not trust the government, the military, the police, or any other institution that represents the central government.[11] People also lacked faith in basic services at the local level. They were dissatisfied with the availability of healthcare services, as well as the quality of water, roads, highways, and affordable housing.

Elections, the foundation of a democracy, have always been marred in Afghanistan by corruption, fraud, and voter intimidation. The level of fraud in the 2014 Afghan presidential election was so significant that more than 850,000 of roughly 7 million ballots were invalidated after months of recounting under the supervision of foreign inspectors and the United Nations.[12] Most recently, it took the Independent Election Commission (IEC) of Afghanistan several months to announce the final results of the 2018 parliamentary elections and 2019 presidential election due to incompetence, corruption, and lack of management by the IEC.[13]

Afghanistan is ranked at the bottom of the Global Law and Order Index, indicating that lawlessness is

---

[10] Zach Bikus, "Inside Afghanistan: Stability in Institutions Remains Elusive," Gallup World Report, 4 September 2019.

[11] Bikus, "Inside Afghanistan."

[12] "Commission Releases Disputed 2014 Afghan Election Results," Reuters, 24 February 2016.

[13] Ali Yawar Adili, *The Results of Afghanistan's 2018 Parliamentary Elections: A New, but Incomplete Wolesi Jirga* (Kabul: Afghanistan Analysts Network, 2020).

widespread in the country.[14] In a recent Gallup survey, only 13 percent of Afghans said they felt safe walking alone at night, and only one in three Afghans had confidence in their local law enforcement. Almost one-half of the respondents said their property had been stolen in the last 12 months.[15] Afghans also have very little confidence in their judicial system, which operates in utter chaos. Corruption is extensive, with judges and lawyers often subject to threats and bribes from local leaders and armed groups.[16]

Given that the United States has spent hundreds of billions of dollars in Afghanistan, it is critical to emphasize how little, if any, progress has been made in the country during the last 20 years. By some estimates, the United States has now spent more on Afghanistan reconstruction efforts than it spent on the Marshall Plan to rebuild Europe after World War II. The purpose of this book is to illustrate how little progress the United States has made in Afghanistan, as well as to focus more attention on the country's economic development diffi-

---

[14] Gallup's Law and Order Index uses four questions to gauge people's sense of personal security and their personal experiences with crime and law enforcement: In the city or area where you live, do you have confidence in the local police force? Do you feel safe walking alone at night in the city or area where you live? Within the last 12 months, have you had money or property stolen from you or another household member? Within the past 12 months, have you been assaulted or mugged? *Global Law and Order, 2020* (Washington, DC: Gallup, 2020). The list of countries along with Afghanistan with the lowest law and order index scores include Gabon, Venezuela, Liberia, South Africa, the Gambia, Uganda, Sierra Leone, Botswana, and Mexico.

[15] R. J. Reinhart and Julie Ray, "Inside Afghanistan: Law and Order Becomes a Casualty of War," Gallup World Report, 19 August 2019.

[16] Reinhart and Ray, "Inside Afghanistan."

culties, despite spending vast sums of money and blood, and make suggestions for how to succeed in Afghanistan now and in the future.

Theoretical Perspective

The term *donor aid* has been defined in a variety of ways by a number of academics. *Foreign aid*, according to Helen V. Milner and Dustin Tingley, "is a transfer of resources" from one country to another as a means of interacting with one another.[17] Kunle Ajayi adds that foreign aid is the type of assistance provided by a government or financial institution to countries that are experiencing difficulties.[18] *Aid*, according to Michael P. Todaro and Stephen C. Smith, is a transfer of capital from industrialized to developing countries.[19] Because it is a contribution, it is expected that the donor will not benefit financially from the donation.

Simbarashe Gukumure outlines a variety of roles that aid plays, including the incentive for affirmative action that the donor finds desirable, as well as infrastructure development. The most prevalent type of help is that which is given for development, namely to alleviate poverty. Foreign aid, on the other hand, serves three purposes: economic, political, and humanitarian. These areas are inextricably linked and reliant on one another.

---

[17] Helen V. Milner and Dustin Tingley, ed, "Introduction to the Geopolitics of Foreign Aid," in *Geopolitics of Foreign Aid*, vol. 1 (Cheltenham, UK: Edward Elgar, 2013).

[18] Kunle Ajayi, *International Administration and Economic Relations in Changing World* (Ilorin, Nigeria: Majab Publishers, 2002).

[19] Michael P. Todaro and Stephen C. Smith, *Economic Development*, 8th ed. (Harlow, UK: Pearson, 2003).

Aid, it is often assumed, promotes development in the recipient country.[20]

The stated purpose of foreign aid is to eradicate extreme poverty around the world. Jerker Carlsson, Gloria Somolekae, and Nicolas van de Walle evaluated aid effectiveness on two fronts. The first was the project's ability to meet its aims and objectives. The second, and most relevant to this study, was how sustainable aid was—that is, the project's potential to achieve positive results over a long period of time once external resources are no longer available or are significantly decreased. As a result, talking about aid without mentioning sustainability is a misnomer.[21]

The flow of resources from affluent, highly industrialized countries to primarily poorer, economically challenged countries can be traced back to the post-World War II reconstruction era. The Marshall Plan's unparalleled success in providing resources from the United States to war-torn Europe has previously convinced authorities that a similar transfer to poverty-stricken

---

[20] Simbarashe Gukumure, "Interrogating Foreign Aid and Sustainable Development Conundrum in African Countries: A Zimbabwean Experience of Debt Trap and Service Delivery," *International Journal of Politics and Good Governance* 3, no. 3.4 (4th quarter, 2012).

[21] Jerker Carlsson, Gloria Somolekae, and Nicolas van de Walle, eds., *Foreign Aid in Africa: Learning from Country Experience* (Uppsala, Sweden: Nordic Africa Institute, 1997).

nations will reproduce this accomplishment.[22] According to Gukumure, a staggering $17.5 billion (USD) was sent to Western European countries to help them recover from the consequences of World War II. The aid phenomenon was a natural outgrowth of the Marshall Plan's modernizing effort. Aid has been a constant part of development discourse and practice since the Marshall Plan was implemented.[23]

Dambisa Moyo recognized that reliance was the primary reason why aid failed in other parts of the world. For example, African governments foster reliance by considering help as ongoing, permanent, and dependable, and by failing to plan adequately in the event that aid is removed. Aid donor nations are just as culpable, because by failing to engage in long-term solutions while ostensibly assisting developing countries, they encourage the notion that aid can be permanent. In such a scenario, poor countries will be trapped in a cycle of dependency.[24]

U.S. Involvement in Afghanistan Post-9/11

Afghanistan has historically been a poor country. The country's contemporary history is marked by monumen-

---

[22] Most development organizations no longer use terms like *Third World* or *developing*. In the World Development Indicators database, the 189 World Bank member countries, plus 28 other economies with populations of more than 30,000, are classified by geographic region, by income group, and by the operational lending categories of the World Bank. See "How Does the World Bank Classify Countries?," World Bank, accessed 15 September 2021.

[23] Gukumure, "Interrogating Foreign Aid and Sustainable Development Conundrum in African Countries."

[24] Dambisa Moyo, *Dead Aid: Why Aid Is Not Working and There Is a Way for Africa* (New York: Farrar, Straus, and Giroux, 2009).

tal battles with the British Empire, the Soviet Union, and many other regional powers. However, the last four decades have been the most tumultuous years by far. The millennial generation of Afghanistan was born into a war that still ravages the country, and there seems to be no end in sight. After the Soviet Union's withdrawal from Afghanistan in 1989, the country plunged into a brutal civil war of the mujahideen that resulted in the uprising of the Taliban movement. In 1995, this Islamic extremist group of newly graduated *madrassa* students took over the majority of the country and declared an Islamic Emirate government.[25]

On their first day in Kabul, the Taliban brutally murdered the former president of Afghanistan, Dr. Najibullah Ahmadzai, and hung him in a traffic circle on a lamppost for the public to see. The civil war had already forced millions of Afghans out to neighboring Pakistan and Iran, and only a small number of people with little means remained under the brutal regime of the Taliban. The country was shattered during the infighting of the mujahideen. Very little was left of government structures and buildings. Roads were destroyed, bridges had collapsed, and schools were demolished. The Taliban were taking over a country that had already been through a violent civil war.[26]

Despite all, the Taliban reigned with a strict Islamic rule and expected people to live as they did in the seventh century of the Prophet Mohammad. Television

---

[25] The term *madrassa* refers to an institution of higher education in the Islamic sciences. "A Historical Timeline of Afghanistan," PBS News Hour, 31 December 2014.

[26] "A Historical Timeline of Afghanistan."

was banned, music was prohibited, playing sports was outlawed, men were forced to grow a beard, and women were not allowed in public unless they were with a male companion. In addition, girls were barred from going to school and people were forced to pray five times a day. Those who violated these strict Taliban rules were punished in public, depending on the severity of the violation, either by lynching, mutilation, or execution in a football stadium full of people on a Friday afternoon after the *jum'ah* prayers.[27]

The author's aunt, who lived during the reign of the Taliban, remembers seeing a woman who was struggling to carry her small child and a load of groceries on a street in Kabul. When her body-length burqa shifted, showing part of her legs, a Talib (member of the Taliban) commander passing by screamed at her and beat her with a strap repeatedly until she fell to ground and could not up.

As a teenager, the author traveled to Afghanistan once during the Taliban regime in the summer of 1999. His father took the family to visit Kabul for a couple of weeks. While living in Pakistan, the author's father had never grown a beard. For him to travel to Afghanistan, he had to have long facial hair, so he tried to grow his beard a couple of weeks before departure. Since it was not yet long enough to pass the Taliban beard test

---

[27] The term *jum'ah* refers to Friday of the Muslim week and the special noon service that all adult, male, free Muslims are required to attend. The jum'ah, which replaces the usual noon ritual prayer (*ṣalāt al-ẓuhr*), must take place before a sizable number of Muslims (according to some legal scholars, 40 Muslims) in a central mosque in each area. "Taliban Territory: Life in Afghanistan under the Militants," BBC News, 8 June 2017.

(i.e., the beard had to be long enough to extend past a clasped fist or fill a standard lantern glass), he had to obtain a letter from an authority figure in the Taliban government stating that the authorities must cooperate with him in spite of the fact that he lacked the standard facial hair.[28] As the author's family entered Kabul, Taliban foot soldiers alongside the road holding flat leathery straps in their hands stopped them, singling out his father to get out of the car. He was then pushed and shoved to the Taliban chief who was sitting on a sofa in the back of a muddy truck for questioning. The rest of the family could not hear what was said, but they could see the father showing them a paper—the letter obtained from the Talib figure explaining his lack of beard. After a quick look at the letter, the soldiers let him go. This happened multiple times as the family traveled from the Torkham border with Pakistan to Kabul. While the author's father was fortunate to have had that letter for protection, others were not as lucky. Some with shorter beards were lynched, kicked, and slapped in full view of the public.[29]

These personal stories offer a small glimpse into the daily life of those living in Afghanistan during the brutal Taliban regime between 1995 and 2001. In addition to these constant harassments and brutal punishments, Afghans suffered terrible economic conditions. The Taliban government was not recognized internationally by any country except for a few Islamic na-

---

[28] "Every Man in Mosul Ordered to Grow a Beard," Radio Free Europe, 29 April 2015.

[29] "Taliban Religious Police Jail Beard-trimmers for 10 days," RAWA News, 18 December 1999.

tions. Initially, Pakistan, Saudi Arabia, and the United Arab Emirates (UAE) recognized the radical group as the legitimate Afghan government, though the UAE would later sever ties with the Taliban in 2001.[30] Consequently, Afghanistan had minimal interaction with the outside world. The domestic economy was nonexistent, and inflation was skyrocketing. People had very little to eat, and public services were subpar or barely existent—there was no electricity, running water, or decent healthcare. People were truly living in the seventh century.[31]

Though Afghans who lived under the Taliban's brutal regime were already at their breaking point, there was little they could do to change the situation. Then, on 11 September 2001 (9/11), the World Trade Center in New York City and the Pentagon outside Washington, DC, were attacked by commercial airplanes hijacked by the terrorist group al-Qaeda, and another flight was overtaken and crashed in the Pennsylvania countryside. While this heinous act killed nearly 3,000 Americans, after the United States and its allies invaded Afghanistan in October 2001, 32 million Afghans were freed from the Taliban's brutality. Within weeks of the invasion, the Taliban regime was defeated, and the country was liberated.[32]

Osama bin Laden, the leader of al-Qaeda and the

---

[30] "United Arab Emirates Won't Recognize Taliban," ABC News, 7 January 2006.

[31] Ahmed Rashid, *Taliban: Militant Islam, Oil and Fundamentalism in Central Asia* (New Haven, CT: Yale University Press, 2010).

[32] *The Global War on Terrorism: The First 100 Days* (Washington, DC: White House, 2001).

mastermind of the 9/11 attacks, was living in Afghanistan at the time. Neither he nor any of the hijackers were citizens of Afghanistan, but the Taliban were complicit in these attacks by giving bin Laden full protection and his terrorist group the ability to operate freely within the boundaries of Afghanistan. This allowed bin Laden to train terrorists and plan attacks on the United States. The United States wanted the Taliban to turn him over, but they denied the request, stating that bin Laden was their guest and it was against "Afghan cultural norms" to hand over a guest to the "infidels" in the United States.[33] The U.S. government then decided to act, with the help of its allies in Europe and Asia, and invaded Afghanistan. It took the American military about four weeks to destroy the Taliban and pave the way for Afghanistan's Northern Alliance to take control of the Afghan capital of Kabul without any resistance from the Taliban.[34] As a sign of solidarity with the United States, 42 other countries decided to engage in the war by sending 65,000 troops to Afghanistan under the umbrella of the International Security Assistance Force (ISAF).[35]

On 18 April 2002, U.S. president George W. Bush, speaking before cadets at the Virginia Military Institute (VMI), outlined America's role in Afghanistan reconstruction. He stated that military might alone would

---

[33] "Afghanistan: Taliban Refuses to Hand over Bin Laden," Radio Free Europe, 21 September 2001.

[34] The Northern Alliance was officially known as the United Islamic Front for the Salvation of Afghanistan. They were a guerrilla group fighting against the Taliban in the north.

[35] "NATO and Afghanistan," North Atlantic Treaty Organization, 6 July 2021; and "The U.S. War in Afghanistan 1999–2021," Council on Foreign Relations, accessed 8 July 2021.

not be enough to deliver "true peace" to Afghanistan
unless the war-torn country rebuilt its roads, health care
system, schools, and businesses, similar to what Europe
and Japan did after World War II ended in 1945.

> *We know that true peace will only be
> achieved when we give the Afghan
> people the means to achieve their own
> aspirations. Peace will be achieved by
> helping Afghanistan develop its own
> stable government. Peace will be achieved
> by helping Afghanistan train and develop
> its own national army. And peace will be
> achieved through an education system for
> boys and girls which works.*[36]

In this speech, the president made it clear that the
United States was prepared to lead an international effort in Afghanistan, invoking the name of U.S. Army
general George C. Marshall Jr., who graduated from
VMI in 1901 and served as President Harry S. Truman's
secretary of state after World War II.

> *By helping to build an Afghanistan that is
> free from this evil and is a better place in
> which to live, we are working in the best
> traditions of George Marshall. Marshall
> knew that our military victory against
> enemies in World War II had to be fol-*

---

[36] A transcript of this speech is available at "President Bush Speaks
at VMI, Addresses Middle East Conflict," CNN Transcripts, 17
April 2002; and James Dao, "A Nation Challenged: The President;
Bush Sets Role for U.S. in Afghan Rebuilding," *New York Times*, 18
April 2002.

lowed by a moral victory that resulted in better lives for individual human beings.[37]

How far have we progressed toward President Bush's postwar reconstruction goals set in 2002 for Afghanistan? After almost two decades, it is critical to assess and comprehend how much the United States has spent in Afghanistan and what has been accomplished as a result of that investment. Further, how can America's efforts toward reconstruction in Afghanistan be compared to that of the Marshall Plan during reconstruction in Europe after World War II?

---

[37] Dao, "A Nation Challenged."

CHAPTER ONE

The European Recovery Program

Wars are bred by poverty and oppression. Continued peace is possible only in a relatively free and prosperous world.

~ George C. Marshall,
U.S. Secretary of State (1947–49)[1]

Imagine a world without governments, institutions, or universities. Money is worthless and banks are abandoned. Shops sit empty and the great factories and businesses that once existed have all been destroyed or dismantled. There is no food. The police force is nonexistent. Men with weapons and knives roam the streets, taking what they want from stores and private properties. People steal what they want without regard for ownership. Goods and food belong to the powerful who can hold on to them and those willing to guard them with their lives. Women sell their bodies for food and protection. People have no access to information. There are no movie theaters and certainly no television. The radio works intermittently, and the population has not seen a newspaper for weeks.

The current generation only sees such a world as a Netflix drama series or a Hollywood film. However, this scene comes from the tragic history of Europe in

---

[1] *The Papers of George Catlett Marshall*, vol. 6, *"The Whole World Hangs in the Balance," January 8, 1947–September 30, 1949* (Baltimore, MD: Johns Hopkins University Press, 2013), 195–97.

the years following the end of World War II. The war was one of the major transformative events of the twentieth century, with 39 million people killed in Europe alone.[2] Vast amounts of physical infrastructure were destroyed, and many people were forced to abandon or hand over their property without any meaningful compensation. Hunger among ordinary citizens was common, even in areas considered relatively prosperous. Families were separated; children lost fathers, mothers, sisters, and brothers. As a result of the war, the political and economic landscape of many European countries changed permanently.

One of the things that was common across Europe in the post-World War II era was the ubiquitous presence of hunger. One might expect that the food situation in Europe would improve once the war was over, but it only got worse. Many American troops were shocked by what they saw when they arrived in Europe after Germany surrendered. They had expected to see destruction and a certain amount of disorganization, but few had anticipated the level of deprivation they encountered. In the months following the declaration of peace, daily rations in Germany fell from 1,400 calories per day to 1,244.[3] In Berlin, children were seen gathering grass from the parks to eat, and tropical fish

---

[2] Iris Kesternich et al., *The Effects of World War II on Economic and Health Outcomes across Europe*, Rand Working Paper Series WR-917 (Santa Monica, CA: Rand, 2012), https://doi.org/10.2139/ssrn .1992007.

[3] Keith Lowe, *Savage Continent: Europe in the Aftermath of World War II* (New York: St. Martin's Press, 2012), 38–39.

from the aquarium were stolen for food.[4] As a result of this mass starvation and malnutrition, the outbreak of diseases was rampant across the continent. Malaria, tuberculosis, and many other infectious diseases resurged, killing thousands of people.[5]

Keith Lowe writes in *Savage Continent: Europe in the Aftermath of World War II* that the problem was not simply a world-wide shortage of food, but that food could not be distributed properly. After six years of war, Europe's transportation infrastructure had been utterly crippled, roads were destroyed, and law and order were nonexistent. For food to reach the most vulnerable and needy populations across Europe, the railway network had to be rebuilt, roads repaired, and law and order restored. In parts of Europe, food supplies were often looted before they arrived at their destination, leaving aid agencies unable to distribute vital necessities of life.[6]

Starvation was one of the most difficult problems in the immediate aftermath of the war. Ray Hunting, a British Army officer, was used to seeing beggars during his travels in the Middle East but was utterly surprised to witness the level of desperation he saw in Europe in 1944. At one point, he threw some of his spare food to a crowd of people surrounding the train in which he was traveling. The crowd fought over the food indiscriminately, turning "into a mass of struggling bodies fighting

---

[4] Lowe, *Savage Continent*, 39.
[5] Frank G. Boudreau, "Nutrition in War and Peace," *Milbank Quarterly* 83, no. 4 (2005): 609–23, https://doi.org/10.1111/j.1468-0009.2005.00394.x.
[6] Lowe, *Savage Continent*, 40.

for the falling gifts. Men punched and kicked each other to gain possession of the tins; women tore food from each other's mouths to push into the hands of children who were in peril of being trampled underfoot in the violence."[7]

The German population suffered from severe hunger between 1945 and 1948. As a result, death rates increased fourfold among adults and tenfold for infants during this period.[8] Based on some accounts, 1 in every 4 adults and 1 in every 10 infants lost their lives during this period in Germany. Since the beginning of the German occupation of Poland in 1939, the food security situation of the non-German population there was even worse. The average nutritional intake for Poles was about 930 calories in 1941, and the situation was magnified in poor localities.[9] In Warsaw ghettos, food rations were limited to approximately 186 calories per day, which is about the same as a regular fast-food cheeseburger today.[10]

Figure 2 illustrates the gross domestic product (GDP) per capita for some of the major European countries involved in the war relative to that of the United States. World War II was quite destructive for the countries involved, especially those on the losing side. Germany lost approximately 46 percent of its GDP per capita between 1938 and 1950, which created a lower standard of living for the entire population. An

---

[7] Lowe, *Savage Continent*.

[8] Lowe, *Savage Continent*.

[9] Kesternich et al., *The Effects of World War II on Economic and Health Outcomes across Europe*, 103–18.

[10] Harold Zink, *The United States in Germany, 1944–1955* (Princeton, NJ: D. Van Nostrand, 1957).

Figure 2. Percent change in per capita GDP, 1938–50

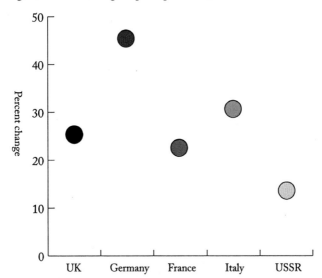

Source: Mark Harrison, ed., *The Economics of World War II: Six Great Powers in International Comparison* (Cambridge, UK: Cambridge University Press, 1998), 1–42, https://doi.org/10.1017/CBO 9780511523632.

average family's income was slashed by half, resulting in mass hunger and despair.[11]

The most dramatic figures highlight the total GDP of Germany between 1940 and 1950 (figure 3). In the early stages of World War II, the total GDP of Germany was about $716 billion (USD). This figure remained steady until 1944, the peak year of the war, when the German economy shrank by almost 40 percent, plum-

---

[11] Kesternich, et al., *The Effects of World War II on Economic and Health Outcomes across Europe*, 103–18.

Figure 3. Total GDP in Germany, inflation adjusted, 1940–50, USD billions

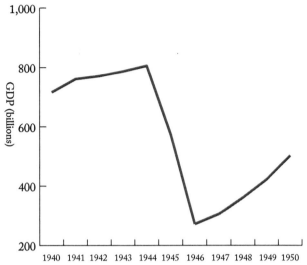

Source: "World Development Indicators: Germany," World Bank.

meting from $806 billion to $574 billion (USD). The German economy continued to dwindle even after the war ended. The country's overall GDP further declined to $272 billion in 1946, illustrating a 196-percent contraction of the economy between 1944 and 1946, just one year after the war ended.[12]

In addition to massive hunger and a dire economic situation, much of Europe lay in ruins, and millions of people were displaced. Germany, at the center of all the destruction, suffered the most damage during the war.

---

[12] "World Development Indicators: Germany," World Bank, accessed 9 July 2021.

Approximately 3.6 million apartments were destroyed by British and American air force bombing raids. These structures accounted for approximately one-fifth of all living spaces in Germany.[13] According to figures from the Reich's Statistical Office, Berlin lost as much as 50 percent of its habitable spaces; Hamburg, 53 percent; and Cologne, 70 percent. The massive destruction throughout Germany rendered approximately 20 million people homeless.[14] They lived in cellars, ruins, holes in the ground, and anywhere they could find shelter. They were deprived of essential services such as water, gas, and electricity. Although the largest numbers of destroyed buildings were apartments, many other public buildings including schools, hospitals, and churches were also razed to the ground or severely damaged.

Life expectancy also continued to decline in Europe throughout the World War II period. Figure 4 depicts the continuous decline in the average number of years a German citizen expected to live during the war. In 1945, the average life expectancy in Germany was 29 years, the lowest in the history of that country. This drastic decline in life expectancy was largely due to the war that had killed millions, but it was also due to increased poverty and a lack of healthcare, sanitation, and water.[15]

Inception of the Marshall Plan
The 1948 European Recovery Plan (also known as the

---

[13] Lowe, *Savage Continent.*
[14] Lowe, *Savage Continent.*
[15] "Life Expectancy (from Birth) from 1875 to 2020," Statista, accessed 9 July 2021.

Figure 4. Life expectancy in Germany, 1940–50

Source: "Life Expectancy (from Birth) from 1875 to 2020," Statista.

Marshall Plan) was developed in the United States out of desperation to save Europe from extreme poverty and to eliminate the spread of Communism across the region as people coped with starvation and other effects of the war. Six years of devastating conflict had battered and staggered Europe economically. The survivors of the war were left with a lack of food and housing. In addition to creating widespread human and infrastructure destruction, the war had also crippled local economies, which in turn resulted in the need for massive imports from the United States and very few exports. The economic imbalance caused the prices for grains, raw materials, and machinery being imported from abroad to increase. This desperate situation was further exacerbated by the fierce winter of 1946–47 and what followed, including crop failures and the worst harvest of the century. The production of necessary food items such as milk, meat, and grains fell by 30 percent during this time.[16] The French government severed the daily bread ration by half to just 200 grams, while the Germans shivered without heat and their GDP plummeted 70 percent between 1945 and 1947.[17] These domestic circumstances led to a wide array of unrest, such as the labor protests seen in Germany and Austria.[18]

Rising prices and declining production not only fueled widespread poverty and negativity among the people, but it also made them more vulnerable and susceptible to political influence by hegemonic powers in the region. Indigenous Communist parties in France, Italy, and Greece had already started to voice their dissatisfaction with capitalism and visions of a better Europe.[19] Greece had been convulsed into a civil war by a Communist-led insurgency supported by neighboring

---

[16] *The State of Food and Agriculture, 1955: Review of a Decade and Outlook* (Rome, Italy: Food and Agriculture Organization, United Nations, 1955).

[17] Barry Machado, "Conceptualizing the Marshall Plan," in *In Search of a Usable Past: The Marshall Plan and Postwar Reconstruction Today* (Lexington, VA: George C. Marshall Foundation, 2007).

[18] Kim Berg, "Demonstrating for Change," Deutschland, 15 July 2019; and Warren Williams, "Flashpoint Austria: The Communist-Inspired Strikes of 1950," *Journal of Cold War Studies* 9, no. 3 (2007): 115–36.

[19] See, for example, Norman M. Naimark, "Stalin and Europe in the Postwar Period, 1945–53: Issues and Problems," *Journal of Modern European History* 2, no. 1 (2004): 28–57.

Communist governments in the Balkans.[20] The spread of Communism to other European countries that had just come out of World War II and were struggling with poverty was imminent. This dire situation provoked an unprecedented action by the United States to counteract the spread of Communism by giving Europeans an alternative through U.S. secretary of state George C. Marshall's vision for the region.

Inspirational speeches at timely moments have played a major role in defining humanity's approach to tackling historic problems. Marshall's speech at Harvard University in 1947 counts as one of those times. It is one of the most eloquent, relatively short speeches to capture the popular imagination of the time.

In his address at Harvard University's 1947 commencement ceremony, Marshall outlined a blueprint for reconstructing a devastated Europe that was only just emerging from World War II through the injection of U.S. foreign assistance on a massive scale. The speech articulately defined U.S. policy toward Europe after the war, which eventually became the cornerstone of the Marshall Plan. The administration of President Harry S. Truman designed the European Recovery Program based on this policy and delivered much-needed help to Europe, costing American taxpayers between $12 and $13 billion.[21]

---

[20] See, for example, Nikos Marantzidis, "The Greek Civil War (1944–1949) and the International Communist System," *Journal of Cold War Studies* 15, no. 4 (2013): 25–54.

[21] George C. Marshall, "Remarks by the Secretary of State at Harvard University on 5 June 1947" (speech, Harvard University, Cambridge, MA, 5 June 1947), hereafter Marshall speech.

I need not tell you, gentlemen, that the world situation is very serious. That must be apparent to all intelligent people. I think one difficulty is that the problem is one of such enormous complexity that the very mass of facts presented to the public by press and radio make it exceedingly difficult for the man in the street to reach a clear appraisement of the situation. Furthermore, the people of this country are distant from the troubled areas of the earth and it is hard for them to comprehend the plight and consequent reactions of the long-suffering peoples, and the effect of those reactions on their governments in connection with our efforts to promote peace in the world.

In considering the requirements for the rehabilitation of Europe, the physical loss of life, the visible destruction of cities, factories, mines and railroads was correctly estimated but it has become obvious during recent months that this visible destruction was probably less serious than the dislocation of the entire fabric of European economy. For the past 10 years, conditions have been highly abnormal. The feverish preparation for war and the more feverish maintenance of the war effort engulfed all aspects of national economies. Machinery has fallen into disrepair or is entirely obsolete. Under the arbitrary

*and destructive Nazi rule, virtually ev-
ery possible enterprise was geared into the
German war machine. Long-standing
commercial ties, private institutions,
banks, insurance companies, and shipping
companies disappeared, through loss of
capital, absorption through nationaliza-
tion, or by simple destruction. In many
countries, confidence in the local currency
has been severely shaken. The breakdown
of the business structure of Europe during
the war was complete. Recovery has been
seriously retarded by the fact that two
years after the close of hostilities a peace
settlement with Germany and Austria
has not been agreed upon. But even given
a more prompt solution of these difficult
problems the rehabilitation of the economic structure of Europe quite evident-
ly will require a much longer time and
greater effort than had been foreseen.*

*There is a phase of this matter which
is both interesting and serious. The farmer
has always produced the foodstuffs to exchange with the city dweller for the other
necessities of life. This division of labor is
the basis of modern civilization. At the
present time it is threatened with breakdown. The town and city industries are
not producing adequate goods to exchange
with the food producing farmer. Raw materials and fuel are in short supply. Ma-*

chinery is lacking or worn out. The farmer or the peasant cannot find the goods for sale which he desires to purchase. So the sale of his farm produce for money which he cannot use seems to him an unprofitable transaction. He, therefore, has withdrawn many fields from crop cultivation and is using them for grazing. He feeds more grain to stock and finds for himself and his family an ample supply of food, however short he may be on clothing and the other ordinary gadgets of civilization. Meanwhile people in the cities are short of food and fuel. So the governments are forced to use their foreign money and credits to procure these necessities abroad. This process exhausts funds which are urgently needed for reconstruction. Thus a very serious situation is rapidly developing which bodes no good for the world. The modern system of the division of labor upon which the exchange of products is based is in danger of breaking down.

The truth of the matter is that Europe's requirements for the next three or four years of foreign food and other essential products—principally from America—are so much greater than her present ability to pay that she must have substantial additional help or face economic, social, and political deterioration of a very grave character.

The remedy lies in breaking the vicious circle and restoring the confidence of the European people in the economic future of their own countries and of Europe as a whole. The manufacturer and the farmer throughout wide areas must be able and willing to exchange their products for currencies the continuing value of which is not open to question.

Aside from the demoralizing effect on the world at large and the possibilities of disturbances arising as a result of the desperation of the people concerned, the consequences to the economy of the United States should be apparent to all. It is logical that the United States should do whatever it is able to do to assist in the return of normal economic health in the world, without which there can be no political stability and no assured peace. Our policy is directed not against any country or doctrine but against hunger, poverty, desperation and chaos. Its purpose should be the revival of a working economy in the world so as to permit the emergence of political and social conditions in which free institutions can exist. Such assistance, I am convinced, must not be on a piecemeal basis as various crises develop. Any assistance that this Government may render in the future should provide a cure rather than a mere palliative. Any government that is willing to assist in the task of recovery will find full co-operation I am sure, on the part of the United States Government. Any government which maneuvers to block the recovery of other countries cannot expect help from us. Furthermore, governments, political parties, or groups which seek to perpetuate human misery in order to profit therefrom politically or otherwise will encounter the opposition of the United States.

It is already evident that, before the United States Government can proceed much further in its efforts to alleviate the situation and help start the European world on its way to recovery, there must be some agreement among the countries of Europe as to the requirements of the situation and the part those countries themselves will take in order to give proper effect to whatever action might be undertaken by this Government. It would be neither fitting nor efficacious for this Government to undertake to draw up unilaterally a program designed to place Europe on its feet economically. This is the business of the Europeans. The initiative, I think, must come from Europe. The role of this country should consist of friendly aid in the drafting of a European program and of later support of such a program so far as it may be practical for us to do so. The

*program should be a joint one, agreed to
by a number, if not all European nations.*

*An essential part of any successful ac-
tion on the part of the United States is an
understanding on the part of the people of
America of the character of the problem
and the remedies to be applied. Political
passion and prejudice should have no part.
With foresight, and a willingness on the
part of our people to face up to the vast
responsibility which history has clearly
placed upon our country, the difficulties I
have outlined can and will be overcome.*[22]

Economists have long debated the extent to which
the Marshall Plan helped the reconstruction and postwar economic growth and prosperity of Western Europe. Some, like Niall Ferguson, have argued whether
to even call this unprecedented economic aid an act of
altruism by the United States.[23] Others believe that the
American government simply wanted to spread capitalism and democracy around the world, while at the same
time limiting the expansion of Communism, through
this generous economic package.[24]

However, what appears beyond dispute is that the
Marshall Plan had a significant impact on the lives of

---

[22] Marshall speech.

[23] Niall Ferguson, "Dollar Diplomacy: How Much Did the Marshall
Plan Really Matter?," *New Yorker*, 20 August 2007.

[24] Michael J. Hogan, *The Marshall Plan: America, Britain, and the
Reconstruction of Western Europe, 1947–1952* (Cambridge, UK:
Cambridge University Press, 1987), https://doi.org/10.1017/CBO
9780511583728.

ordinary Europeans who were living in a dire situation after the most destructive war in modern history. The U.S. aid package gave them the economic boost they desperately needed, while also undoubtedly contributing to the development of a new political and economic system in Western Europe that was more or less aligned with America's vision for the continent. One can even argue that the seeds of a united Europe were sown in the years immediately following World War II, when a group of Western European political leaders—including Jean Monnet and Robert Schuman of France, Alcide De Gasperi of Italy, and Konrad Adenaur of Germany—combined a vision of an integrated Europe with support for an American plan of economic recovery and institutional reform.[25] Above all, while the help was provided by the United States, the development programs that encompassed the European Recovery Program were designed and owned by the Europeans.

The Marshall Plan has become a model for economic development in postwar countries around the world. Most recently in Afghanistan and Iraq, such plans were implemented in the hopes that they could accomplish what the Marshall Plan did so successfully in Western Europe. Nearly 75 years after the introduction of the plan, it lives on as a model for underdeveloped countries on how to transition from state socialism to open market economies. This applies particularly to Afghanistan, as the Soviet Union's invasion in the 1980s left the country's institutions heavily dependent on the state. J. Bradford DeLong and Barry Eichengreen write that

---

[25] John Agnew and J. Nicholas Entrikin, eds., *The Marshall Plan Today: Model and Metaphor* (New York: Routledge, 2004), 3.

the Marshall Plan was a unique response to a particular historical circumstance, but their key insight that a market economy needs institutional and policy support to function effectively is as timely today as it was then.[26]

Total Aid Package

The Marshall Plan was in place from April 1948 to September 1951.[27] Initially, when the United States asked European leaders to gather in Paris in the summer of 1947 to map out an economic recovery program, foreign ministers from 16 countries convened a conference to flesh out a concrete program for European rehabilitation and unification. They agreed on a $19 billion aid package effective for four years.[28] Their final report, however, was rejected due to a lack of tangible plans for implementation. President Truman instead asked the U.S. Congress for $17 billion over four years: $6.8 billion for the first 15 months beginning in April 1949 and $10.2 billion for the remaining three years. The participating countries also received $11.8 billion as grants. The total amount of Marshall Plan aid came to $13 billion, which equates to about $138.8 billion in 2019 purchasing power after adjusting for inflation.[29]

[26] J. Bradford DeLong and Barry Eichengreen, "The Marshall Plan: History's Most Successful Structural Adjustment Program" (paper presented at the Centre for Economic Performance and Landeszentralbank Hamburg Conference on Post-World War II European Reconstruction, Hamburg, Germany, 5–7 September 1991); and Agnew and Entrikin, *The Marshall Plan Today*.

[27] Agnew and Entrikin, *The Marshall Plan Today*, 13.

[28] *The Marshall Plan: Lessons Learned for the 21st Century* (Paris: OECD Publishing, 2008), https://doi.org/10.1787/9789264044258-en.

[29] Curt Tarnoff, *The Marshall Plan: Design, Accomplishments, and Significance* (Washington, DC: Congressional Research Service, 2018).

Figure 5. Percentage of Marshall Plan aid distribution, 1948–51

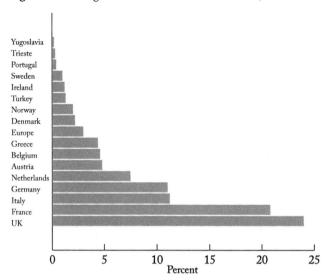

Source: *The Marshall Plan: Lessons Learned for the 21st Century* (Paris: OECD Publishing, 2008), 14, https://doi.org/10.1787/9789264044258-en.

Figure 5 better illustrates the amount of aid money distributed across the 16 participating countries. The top four Marshall Plan aid recipient countries were the United Kingdom (which accounted for roughly 24 percent of individual country totals), France (21 percent), and West Germany and Italy (with 11 percent each). Roughly 66 percent of total economic aid was distributed among these four countries.[30] While Yugoslavia was not included in the Marshall Plan, American economic

---

[30] Agnew and Entrikin, *The Marshall Plan Today*, 14.

aid was transmitted to its government via the Economic Cooperation Act in 1950.[31]

In 1948, the U.S. Congress created a new agency called the Economic Cooperation Administration (ECA) to implement the Marshall Plan.[32] The ECA was given a certain level of autonomy to implement the program without the usual bureaucratic hurdles. A regional office was located in Paris to coordinate the programs of individual countries and to obtain critical European perspectives on implementation. In addition to this office, each country's administrator was assigned to monitor the effectiveness of recovery efforts closely, without infringing on the national sovereignty of host countries. As required by the Marshall Plan legislation, the United States had to sign bilateral agreements with each aid recipient country in which certain commitments from the host country were outlined to meet the objectives of the recovery program, such as steps to stabilize the currency and increase production, as well as obligations to provide economic information to support the evaluation of the program.[33]

The Marshall Plan Programs
The program was mapped into four major components of grants (i.e., commodity assistance, reconstruction efforts, and technical assistance), loans, guaranties, and

---

[31] Tarnoff, *The Marshall Plan*, 8.

[32] Tarnoff, *The Marshall Plan*.

[33] Tarnoff, *The Marshall Plan*.

counterpart funds.[34] Each of these components, which are detailed below, was considered a vital tool for achieving the overarching goal of alleviating poverty and providing a better future for Europeans who had just come out of a terrible war.

THE DOLLAR AID PACKAGE

Due to extreme hunger and poverty in Europe, the ECA initially provided grants to aid recipient countries to purchase food and raw materials. The dollar aid program was designed to supply immediate food-related goods such as food, animal feed, fertilizer, and fuel. According to William Adams Brown Jr. and Redvers Opie, food and materials made up more than 30 percent of the total Marshall Plan program between 1948 and 1951 (figure 6).[35] The ECA provided outright grants that were used to pay for the cost of freight of essential commodities and services mostly from the United States. The program design evolved over time as Europeans' needs changed. The program transitioned from supplying immediate food-related goods to eventually providing mostly raw materials and production equipment.

In subsequent years, food-related aid declined from roughly 50 percent to 27 percent, but the proportion of raw material and machinery assistance increased by

---

[34] William Adams Brown Jr. and Redvers Opie, *American Foreign Assistance* (Washington, DC: Brookings Institution, 1953); and Robert T. Mack, *Raising the World's Standard of Living: The Coordination and Effectiveness of Point Four, United Nations Technical Assistance, and Related Programs* (New York: Citadel Press, 1953), 247.

[35] Brown and Opie, *American Foreign Assistance*; and Mack, *Raising the World's Standard of Living*.

Figure 6. Aid distribution, 1948–51

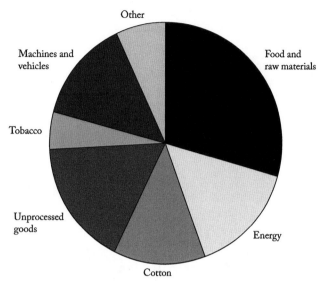

Source: *The Marshall Plan: Lessons Learned for the 21st Centu-ry* (Paris: OECD Publishing, 2008), 17, https://doi.org/10.1787/9789264044258-en.

30 percent during 1949 and 1950.[36] The equipment purchases amounted to $1.4 billion (14 percent) of the total Marshall Plan aid package. This may not seem like a lot, but the aid program helped jump-start Europe's industrial sector. The Marshall Plan partially financed 143 industrial equipment plants. The total cost was $2.25 billion (USD), of which only $565 million was provided by Marshall Plan assistance funds. Twenty-seven other projects focused on power production, and

[36] Harry Baynard Price, *The Marshall Plan and Its Meaning* (New York: Cornell University Press, 1955), 96; and Agnew and Entrikin, *The Marshall Plan Today.*

32 more were involved in the modernization and expansion of steel and iron production. The remaining funds were allocated for the rehabilitation of the transportation infrastructure.[37]

THE COUNTERPART FUNDS

The Marshall Plan required each aid recipient country to match U.S. grant contributions dollar for dollar. These counterpart funds were established as a vehicle for each country to contribute a dollar's worth of its currency for each dollar of grant aid given by the United States. The participating country's matched contribution was placed in this pooled funding for infrastructure development projects such as roads, power plants, housing projects, and airports.

By the end of 1951, approximately $8.6 billion (USD) of counterpart funds had been raised, of which $7.6 billion had been appropriated for use. Roughly $4.8 billion of the total funds was earmarked for investment in utilities, transportation, communication facilities, electric power projects, railroads, agriculture, manufacturing, coal mining, and low-cost housing facilities (figure 7). The remaining $2.8 billion was used for debt reduction in the United Kingdom to help balance its budget. As much as $1 billion in counterpart funds was never released by the ECA.[38]

TECHNICAL ASSISTANCE

The Marshall Plan also provided technical assistance to

---

[37] *The Department of State Bulletin*, vol. 28 (14 January 1952).
[38] Tarnoff, *The Marshall Plan*.

Figure 7. Counterpart funds allocations, 1948–51

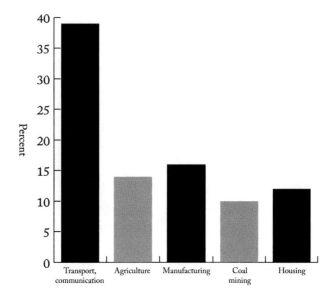

Source: *The Marshall Plan: Lessons Learned for the 21st Century* (Paris: OECD Publishing, 2008), 17, https://doi.org/10.1787/9789264044258-en.

participating countries.[39] As part of the technical assistance program, a special fund was created to finance expenses for U.S. experts in Europe and provide technical workshops to European delegations visiting the United States. The funds from this program were aimed at projects contributing directly to increased productivity.

---

[39] James M. Silberman and Charles Weiss Jr., *Restructuring for Productivity: The Technical Assistance Program of the Marshall Plan as a Precedent for the Former Soviet Union*, Industry Series Paper No. 64 (Washington, DC: World Bank, 1992).

Production was not merely a function of having world-class machinery, but also possessing management skills and labor styles that would operate efficiently. To bring production up to speed, the ECA funded research on business styles, conducted management seminars, and arranged visits of business and labor representatives to the United States to explain American methods of production. The program targeted production problems in the areas of marketing, agriculture, transportation, and communications.

By the end of the Marshall Plan program in 1951, more than $30 million had been spent on the technical assistance program. More than 6,000 Europeans representing a wide variety of economic sectors had come to the United States for training, and about 2,100 American experts had traveled to Europe to provide technical expertise.[40]

INVESTMENT GUARANTIES

The U.S. Congress had authorized $300 million for an investment guaranties program. This portion of the Marshall Plan was designed to encourage American businesses to invest in the modernization and development of European industries by ensuring that they would not lose money when converting their profits from local European notes to U.S. dollars. The program provided assurance to businesses by covering their actual investment earnings or profits up to 175 percent of dollar investment.[41]

---

[40] *The Department of State Bulletin* (14 January 1952).
[41] Tarnoff, *The Marshall Plan.*

Effectiveness of the Programs

These four programs directly contributed to the overarching goal of the Marshall Plan, which was to help alleviate poverty in Europe after the end of World War II. Each component complemented another to achieve the most optimal outcome for the people affected. For instance, while most of the goods shipped to Europe were not distributed as gifts to the general population, raw material was used to produce a final product, which end consumers had to buy in the market at regular price. These goods were sold through private channels, either directly or through the recipient governments. The proceeds from the sales were then put into the counterpart funds for infrastructure development.[42]

Most trade relations in Europe after the war were bilateral due to the nontransferable or nonconvertible nature of their currencies. All payments for imports and exports had to be honored in gold or U.S. dollars. Due to a serious shortage of this currency, countries had to adopt a barter system of exchange to balance their payments with each of the trading countries. This type of trade relations was considered a major obstacle for growth in Europe. The fact that countries tended to balance their payments with each of their trade partners individually inhibited them from choosing the best products at the best prices.[43]

To overcome bilateral trade and payment practices, the Intra-European Payments Agreement was developed

---

[42] Agnew and Entrikin, *The Marshall Plan Today*, 95.

[43] For more information about European integration, see Brown and Opie, *American Foreign Assistance*, 270–312; and Greg Behrman, *The Most Noble Adventure: The Marshall Plan and the Time When America Helped Save Europe* (New York: Free Press, 2007), 262–82.

in 1949. This payment system allowed intra-European purchases to take place without any of the former hurdles. The Intra-European Payments Agreement was heavily dependent on Marshall Plan aid. These purchases were financed through a conditional aid mechanism in which a debtor country could use its purchasing power rights on its creditor's conditional aid portion to finance its supplies. The creditor country would receive conditional aid to pay for the debtor country's supplies, while the latter country received the goods for free. The main purpose of the Marshall Plan was to encourage these types of intra-European exchanges of goods for their economies to grow rather than import goods directly from the United States.[44]

Aid to Europe was not a new development. Americans had contributed roughly $11 billion—more than $100 billion by today's estimation—to Europe between July 1945 and December 1947, in the immediate aftermath of World War II, compared to the Marshall Plan's estimated $13 billion from 1948 to 1951.[45] The former aid package, which was distributed on an ad hoc basis, made no significant difference in European recovery because the programs lacked a coherent approach. The Marshall Plan, meanwhile, was a well-thought-out approach to a dire situation in Europe that included increased agricultural and industrial production, finance reform, and the stimulation of intra-European and international trade. The Marshall Plan ensured that aid

---

[44] Tarnoff, *The Marshall Plan*; and *Intra-European Payments Plan, 1948–49* (Washington, DC: World Bank, 1950).
[45] Gerald Zarr, "The Marshall Plan: Rebuilding a Devastated Europe," *History Magazine*, October/November 2012.

money was spent on both technical support and financial assistance, which would contribute directly to the long-term development of the participating countries.

Further, the Marshall Plan was a joint effort by European nations and the United States. It was owned by the aid recipient countries, as they were heavily involved in the planning and implementation of its every component.[46] It also had a definite timeframe and monetary limits. The U.S. Congress had ensured that a specific amount of money would be appropriated for the program within a set timeframe of 3.5 years. These unique features of the Marshall Plan made it extremely successful in delivering on its main objectives.

Achievements of the Marshall Plan

The post-World War II economic development of Europe is unquestionably the most astonishing recovery in modern history. Few can argue the fact that economic growth in European countries following the implementation of the Marshall Plan was extraordinary. The magnitude of this growth is made clear in the following graphs, which highlight steady growth in macroeconomic indicators of major European countries that participated in the program. While it may be difficult to draw a direct connection between American aid and the economic growth that followed, for the most part, the Marshall Plan served as a stimulus that triggered a chain of events leading to the accomplishments highlighted below.

As figures 8 and 9 show, Germany's GDP per capita,

---

[46] "History of the Marshall Plan," George C. Marshall Foundation, accessed 15 June 2021.

Figure 8. GDP per capita, yearly growth pre- and post-World War II, by percentage

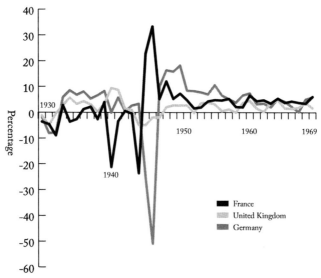

Source: "World Development Indicators: Germany, France, and Great Britain," World Bank.

which is a measure of its total output divided by the total population, increased from -25 percent in 1945 to 16 percent in 1948, when the first Marshall Plan aid package was delivered to the war-torn, economically devastated country.[47] In France, GDP per capita increased by about 70 percent compared to the pre-1914 trend and showed a 100-percent increase from the interwar period of 1939–45.[48] Even the United Kingdom, which experienced the smallest relative acceleration in growth

---

[47] "World Development Indicators."
[48] "World Development Indicators."

Figure 9. Income per person, 1930–70

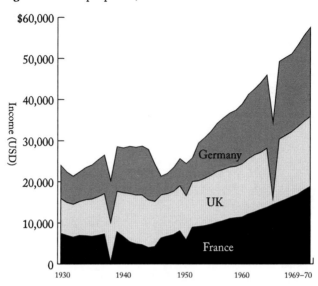

Source: "GDP per Capita, Constant PPP [Purchasing Power Parity] Dollars, v. 27," Gapminder, 2017.

of these three countries after World War II, had a GDP of 20–30 percent above the pre-1914 levels and 30–40 percent compared to the interwar period.[49] By 1960, the production levels for all the participating countries was higher than the best interwar performance. Economic recovery went well beyond the expectations of many who made predictions by extrapolating pre-World War II trends into the future.

Similarly, the average income per person in Germany, which is yet another indicator of how well the

---

[49] "World Development Indicators."

Figure 10. Growth in European production, 1938–51

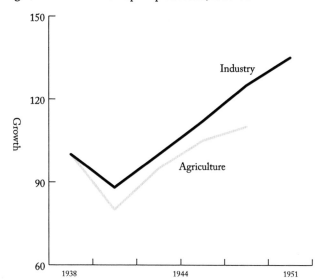

Source: William Adams Brown Jr. and Redvers Opie, *American Foreign Assistance* (Washington, DC: Brookings Institution, 1953).

country's economy recovered, grew by 16.7 percent in 1948 and continued to grow by 15–17 percent in the following years.[50] The average income per person in France increased by 12.2 percent in 1948 and continued to expand by 5–7 percent in consecutive years. Figure 9 is a good illustration of this phenomenon.[51]

One of the main objectives of the Marshall Plan was to increase the aggregate production levels of participating countries. Figure 10 shows how production

---

[50] "GDP per Capita, Constant PPP Dollars, v. 27," Gapminder, 2017.
[51] "GDP per Capita, Constant PPP Dollars, v. 27."

levels compare with prewar trends. By the end of the Marshall Plan in 1951, industrial production for all countries was 35 percent higher than the 1938 prewar level, far exceeding the goal of the program.[52] The growth in industrial production was quite impressive after the mid-1947 dip, and then showed a steep rise onward. By the end of 1951, industrial production levels were 55 percent higher than only four years earlier.[53] The aggregate agricultural production levels increased by nearly 37 percent after 1948. Overall, the total average national production for all 16 countries participating in the program rose by about 33 percent during the four years of the Marshall Plan.[54]

Expanding international trade and tackling trade imbalances among the European countries was yet another goal of the Marshall Plan, which sought to help the countries reach the point where they could pay for their own imports. The objective was for them to be able to pay for 83 percent of their imports through trade with other countries. By the end of 1951, despite a substantial increase in trade volume from the rest of the world, participating countries could pay for 50 percent of their imports.[55]

As a result, European economies opened up, which led to the successful export performance of Western Europe. The sum of their exports plus imports, measured as a share of the total national product, was easily twice that of the interwar average. World War II marked a

[52] Brown and Opie, *American Foreign Assistance.*

[53] Brown and Opie, *American Foreign Assistance.*

[54] *The Department of State Bulletin*, vol. 82 (June 1982), 17.

[55] Tarnoff, *The Marshall Plan.*

period in which international trade was nearly halted, as well as a time in which market liberalization led to massive trade increases not only in its absolute volume but relative to GDP.[56]

This trade expansion allowed for the European economies to grow faster. According to Jeffrey A. Frankel and David Romer, each dollar of expanded exports grows the total national product by approximately $0.34 (USD).[57] Exports allow for an economy to move labor into the export sectors, where it is more productive. It raises consumer welfare and producer productivity by giving consumers more power to purchase imports from other countries. In turn, trade puts pressure on domestic monopolies to decrease prices and to become more efficient, leading to more technological advancements.[58]

Finally, while some achievements of the Marshall Plan are quite tangible, others are not as easily quantifiable, such as the psychological boost it gave to the Europeans and the economic integration of the European continent that ensued from the program.

---

[56] Tarnoff, *The Marshall Plan.*

[57] Jeffrey A. Frankel and David Romer, *Trade and Growth: An Empirical Investigation*, NBER Working Paper No. 5476 (Cambridge, MA: National Bureau of Economic Research, 1996), https://doi.org/10.3386/w5476.

[58] J. Bradford DeLong, "Post-World War II Western European Exceptionalism: The Economic Dimension," in Agnew and Entrikin, *The Marshall Plan Today*, 41.

CHAPTER TWO

The Marshall Plan 2.0

Afghanistan

To most people in the outside world, Afghanistan was an unfamiliar country prior to the terrorist attacks against the United States on 11 September 2001 (9/11). The image of the World Trade Center in New York City being hit by airplanes remains a vivid memory for the author, who was in middle school and doing homework before dinner on that fateful day. His family was living as refugees in Peshawar, Pakistan, at the time and had a guest over from Afghanistan when the local Pakistani news channels suddenly shifted to a live CNN (Cable News Network) broadcast, which was unusual, that showed planes crashing into the towers.[1]

The author did not understand what exactly was happening, but he knew something critical was occurring in the United States, where two of his uncles lived with their families in Boston, Massachusetts. When the author's father returned from work, he turned on the old radio to listen to BBC (British Broadcasting Corporation) Pashto, the primary source of news for most Afghan refugees who were not fully fluent in the local Pakistani language.[2] As days passed, reports emerged about al-Qaeda leader Osama bin Laden's in-

---

[1] "Terror Attacks Hit U.S.," CNN, 11 September 2001.
[2] "US Rocked by Terror Attacks," BBC News, 11 September 2001.

volvement in the attacks as well as the Taliban's complicity.[3]

The author's interest in how the United States would retaliate against bin Laden and the Taliban was piqued. His father had often discussed that if the Taliban were removed from power in Afghanistan, the family might return to Kabul and start a new life there. They would no longer be forced to live as *muhajir*, refugees in a foreign country.[4]

On 7 October 2001, the United States embarked on its longest war in history by launching Operation Enduring Freedom (OEF) in Afghanistan. President George W. Bush uttered the following words in his address to the nation: "On my orders, the United States military has begun strikes against Al Qaida [*sic*] terrorist training camps and military installations of the Taliban regime in Afghanistan."[5] With the full assistance of the British armed forces, the U.S. military initiated a bombing campaign in Afghanistan, officially launching America's operation against the Taliban and al-Qaeda.[6]

---

[3] "Who Is Osama Bin Laden?," BBC News, 18 September 2001.

[4] *Muhajir* is an Arabic term for refugees. The word was widely used by Pakistanis to refer to refugees who had fled wars in Afghanistan and settled in various cities in Pakistan. The word had a demeaning connotation associated with it, highlighting the lower status of an individual in a society.

[5] The full transcript of this speech is available at "Bush Announces Strikes Against Taliban," *Washington Post*, 7 October 2001; and George W. Bush, *Decision Points* (New York: Random House, 2010), 162.

[6] "The U.S. War in Afghanistan, 1999–2021," Council on Foreign Relations, accessed 12 July 2021.

For the first time in its history, the North Atlantic Treaty Organization (NATO) invoked Article 5, committing its members to stand with the United States in its response to the 9/11 attacks.[7] Canada, Australia, Germany, and France pledged their full support in the fight. The goal of OEF was outlined by Bush in his address to the nation: to crush the Taliban, which had seized control of Afghanistan, and to wipe out al-Qaeda.[8] After 20 years, the war in Afghanistan has taken its toll at a cost of nearly $1 trillion (USD), 3,594 U.S. troops killed, and more than 20,000 injured.[9] Four U.S. presidents—George W. Bush, Barack H. Obama, Donald J. Trump, and Joseph R. Biden Jr.—have all engaged in this war with distinct approaches to untangle a complex web

---

[7] Suzanne Daley, "After the Attacks: The Alliance; For First Time, NATO Invokes Joint Defense Pact with U.S.," *New York Times*, 13 September 2001.

[8] Al-Qaeda was the group that planned the 9/11 attacks and successfully executed it using 19 terrorists, most of whom were citizens of Saudi Arabia. *The 9/11 Commission Report: Final Report of the National Commission on Terrorist Attacks upon the United States* (Washington, DC: National Commission on Terrorist Attacks upon the United States, 2004).

[9] Fred Kaplan, "The War in Afghanistan Was Doomed from the Start," *Slate* (blog), 9 December 2019. Based on the author's research, the *direct cost* of the war is approximately $1 trillion. The *indirect cost* of the war, which includes interest on the amount borrowed for the war in Afghanistan as well as veterans' care until 2050, is about another $1 trillion. If the indirect cost is included in the analysis, the total cost of the war is closer to $2 trillion. However, the focus here is on the direct cost of the war and the $1 trillion figure will be used throughout as a result. For more information, see "Costs of War," Watson Institute for International and Public Affairs, Brown University, August 2021.

of challenges and to help develop the impoverished nation. This chapter and chapter 3 discuss Bush's predicament with the war in Afghanistan. He began the fight in the hopes of improving homeland security and bringing peace and prosperity to Afghanistan but fell short of achieving that goal by the time he left office in 2009.[10] Chapter 4 extensively examines Obama's approach to the war and nation-building efforts in Afghanistan. Chapter 5 outlines the human toll and the monetary cost of the war during the last two decades. Finally, chapter 6 deliberates on Trump and Biden's approach to Afghanistan and their efforts to strike a peace deal with the Taliban.

The Bush Doctrine

In his memoir, *Decision Points*, President Bush devotes an entire chapter to Afghanistan and his administration's strategy for the war and nation-building efforts there. He writes, "Twelve days after I announced the start of the war, the first of the Special Forces teams finally touched down."[11] Within days, almost all of the major cities under Taliban rule fell to Coalition forces, including the capital of Kabul.[12] The Afghan people were liberated from the brutality of the Taliban regime. Women came out of their homes without any fear, men shaved their beards, children flew kites or played soc-

---

[10] *The Global War on Terrorism: The First 100 Days* (Washington, DC: White House, 2001).

[11] Bush, *Decision Points*, 170.

[12] Walter L. Perry and David Kassing, *Toppling the Taliban: Air-Ground Operations in Afghanistan, October 2001–June 2002* (Santa Monica, CA: Rand, 2015), https://doi.org/10.7249/RR381.

cer, and everyone welcomed the foreign forces led by the United States through the streets of Mazari Sharif, Herat, Kabul, and many other cities. They were considered liberators who came to save them from the cruelty of the Taliban.[13]

The stronghold of Kandahar was the only city where the Taliban resisted and made an offer to discuss delivering Osama bin Laden to a third country for trial if the United States provided evidence of his involvement in the 9/11 attacks.[14] The White House rejected the offer. After a full airstrike campaign, the Taliban gave up Kandahar on 7 December 2001, two months after OEF began.[15]

One of the strongest elements of Bush's initial war campaign was the creation of a united international Coalition against the war on terrorism. In his book, Bush writes:

> *We would not act alone. [U.S. secretary of state] Colin Powell had done an impressive job rallying countries to our coalition. Some, such as Great Britain and Australia, offered to deploy forces. Others, including Japan and South Korea, pledged humanitarian aid and logistical support. South Korea later sent troops. Key Arab partners, such as Jordan and Saudi Ara-*

[13] Kathy Gannon, "After 17 Years, Many Afghans Blame US for Unending War," AP News, 13 November 2018.

[14] "Bush Rejects Taliban Offer to Hand Bin Laden Over," *Guardian*, 14 October 2001.

[15] George W. Bush, "Presidential Return," C-SPAN, 14 October 2001, 3:18 min.

> *bia, shared sensitive intelligence on al Qaeda's operations.*[16]

Most NATO nations also offered troops for the initial war effort, including Germany, Turkey, Italy, and the Netherlands.[17]

Now that Afghanistan was liberated from the Taliban and its central government—if that even existed—had collapsed, the United States was put in the position to revive a country destroyed by three decades of internal war and marred by extreme poverty.[18] The level of poverty and destruction came as a surprise to most in Washington, DC.[19] Most watched from afar as, during the civil war and the Taliban reign that ensued, the Afghan economy came to a standstill and access to basic services was extremely limited. Afghans had become overly reliant on neighboring countries for basic necessities, and they depended on food aid delivered by humanitarian agencies. The country's institutions, infrastructure, roads, bridges, hospitals, and schools had all but been destroyed during these tumultuous years of war.[20] To establish a governing structure, the United Nations (UN) hosted the Bonn Conference in Germany

---

[16] Bush, *Decision Points*, 164.

[17] Vincent Morelli and Paul Belkin, *NATO in Afghanistan: A Test of the Transatlantic Alliance* (Washington, DC: Congressional Research Service, 2009).

[18] Donald P. Wright et al., *A Different Kind of War: The United States Army in Operation Enduring Freedom (OEF), October 2001– September 2005* (Fort Leavenworth, KS: Combat Studies Institute Press, U.S. Army Combined Arms Center, 2010).

[19] Perry and Kassing, *Toppling the Taliban*.

[20] *The Cost of War: Afghan Experiences of Conflict, 1978–2009* (Kabul: Afghanistan Civil Society Forum, 2009).

in December 2001.[21] A diverse group of Afghans were invited to this conference, including the Northern Alliance, which was made up of Tajiks, Uzbeks, and other ethnic minorities who had some control over much of the country as the Taliban fled.[22] The Rome group was represented by a delegation of the former king of Afghanistan, Mohammad Zahir Shah, while the Peshawar group was led by Afghan refugees living in Pakistan.[23] The UN played a key role in building consensus among these groups of Afghans on certain measures about the future government of their country. After nine days of deliberation, the participants agreed on an ambitious three-year political and administrative plan and chose Hamid Karzai as chairman of an interim authority for six months. Karzai was tasked to convene a *loya jirga*

---

[21] Mark Fields and Ramsha Ahmed, *A Review of the 2001 Bonn Conference and Application to the Road Ahead in Afghanistan* (Washington, DC: Institute for National Strategic Studies, National Defense University, 2011); and "Security Council Endorses Afghanistan Agreement on Interim Arrangements Signed Yesterday in Bonn, Unanimously Adopting Resolution 1383," press release, United Nations Security Council, 12 June 2001. UNSCR 1383 states that the UN is "reaffirming its strong commitment to the sovereignty, independence, territorial integrity and national unity of Afghanistan; Stressing the inalienable right of the Afghan people themselves freely to determine their own political future; Determined to help the people of Afghanistan to bring to an end the tragic conflicts in Afghanistan and promote national reconciliation, lasting peace, stability and respect for human rights, as well as to cooperate with the international community to put an end to the use of Afghanistan as a base for terrorism."

[22] See "Northern Alliance," in Jan Palmowski, *A Dictionary of Contemporary World History*, 3d ed. (Oxford, UK: Oxford University Press, 2008), https://doi.org/10.1093/acref/9780199295678.001.0001.

[23] Tom Heneghan, "Afghans Get Down to Details in UN Talks," Reuters, 28 November 2001.

(grand council) that would then select a transitional government, which in turn would draft a new constitution and hold free and fair elections in the next two years.[24]

Additionally, the participants of the Bonn Conference requested that the United States make a long-term commitment to Afghanistan in the form of strategic partnership and maintain a military force in the country beyond 2014. The agreement also requested U.S. funding of the Afghan National Security Forces (ANSF) through 2015. As part of this pact, the UN authorized the International Security Assistance Force (ISAF) to provide security support to Afghans, and the United Kingdom agreed to lead the force initially. ISAF was one of the largest coalitions in history, with more than 130,000 troops from 51 NATO and partner nations operating in Afghanistan to maintain security.[25]

As soon as the interim government was established and Karzai was sworn in as its head, the author's father decided that it was time for the family to return to Kabul. No one would call them *muhajir* again. It was a new beginning for all Afghans, who now had access to the lives that they could never have had as refugees. In the spring of 2002, the author's family hired a truck from Peshawar to move them back to Kabul. The journey to the Tor-Kham border was easy and full of joy and laughter. After crossing the border into Afghanistan, the sheer destruction of the roads, buildings, and houses was shocking. The truck that had begun the 10-hour

---

[24] Fields and Ahmed, *A Review of the 2001 Bonn Conference and Application to the Road Ahead in Afghanistan.*

[25] "ISAF's Mission in Afghanistan (2001–2014) (Archived)," North Atlantic Treaty Organization, 1 September 2015.

Figure 11. More than 400 Afghan refugee children wait at the Aschiana school in Kabul for clothing and school supplies

Source: official U.S. Navy photo by MC1 Chris Fahey, NATO Training Mission-Afghanistan.

journey from Pakistan with a smooth ride now wobbled like a pendulum as it made its way across massive craters in the road. Men, women, and children wore haunted expressions, with most looking malnourished and physically worn (figure 11). Signs of war were visible everywhere—houses were razed to the ground, broken and abandoned tanks sat on the sides of the road, and bullet holes raked across metal rooftops (figure 12).

The author's family home in Kabul had been destroyed during the war, so they stayed at their grandparents' house, as the grandparents were living in the United States at the time. The house was still erect but visibly battered. The windows, doors, and any wooden material used in the house had been broken or stolen. Even the wires inside the concrete walls had been

Figure 12. The remains of Darul Aman Palace in Kabul, Afghanistan

Source: photo courtesy of Ninaras.

ripped out. People were selling copper wire to make a living. Bullet holes riddled the building. It required a lot of effort to make the house livable again—it needed new windows, cement on the walls to cover the bullet holes, new wiring, paint, trash removal, and, most importantly, a new well because a severe drought during the last decade had dried out the previous one.

This repatriation story mirrors those of millions of Afghans who took the same journey following the toppling of the Taliban regime. According to the United Nations High Commissioner for Refugees (UNHCR), between 2001 and 2004 more than 3.5 million Afghan refugees living in Pakistan and 2.3 million living in Iran returned to their home country.[26] To help with the process, the UN paid each family returning from Pakistan

---

[26] "Global Trends: Forced Displacement in 2018," UNHCR, 20 June 2019.

or Iran a certain amount of money to cover transportation costs. This major influx of refugees caught UN agencies tasked with assisting in their resettlement by surprise. In one report, they indicate that their estimated projection for the repatriation of Afghans was surpassed by 300 percentage points.[27] The largest and most complex operation ever undertaken by UNHCR had previously been in Africa, where 1.7 million Mozambicans returned from six neighboring countries during a four-year period (1992–96).[28] The Afghan operation was three times larger and more complex than that. Figure 13 illustrates the arrival trends of refugees from 2002 to 2008.

This massive influx from voluntary repatriation was a sign of desperation from most Afghans living in refugee camps in Pakistan and Iran. They just wanted to return to their home country and build a simple life like their parents and grandparents had before them. They no longer wanted to be called *muhijir* in Pakistan or *Afghan kaseef* (dirty Afghan) in Iran.

President Bush writes in his book that

> *over time, the thrill of liberation gave way to the daunting task of helping the Afghans rebuild—or, more accurately, build from scratch. Afghanistan in 2001 was the world's third poorest country. Less than 10 percent of the population had access to health care. Four out of every five*

---

[27] David Turton and Peter Marsden, *Taking Refugees for a Ride?: The Politics of Refugee Return*, Issues Paper Series (Kabul: Afghanistan Research and Evaluation Unit, 2002).

[28] Inspection and Evaluation Service, "Evaluation of UNHCR's Repatriation Operation to Mozambique," UNHCR, 1 February 1996.

Figure 13. Annual refugee arrivals, 2002–8, in millions

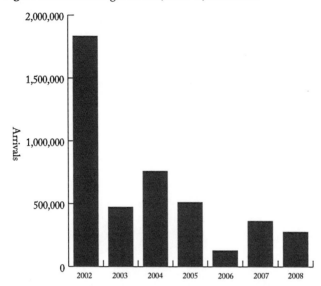

Source: "UNHCR Afghanistan: Voluntary Repatriation, Response Snapshot (1 January–31 July 2019)," UNHCR, 6 August 2019.

women were illiterate. While Afghanistan's land area and population were similar to those of Texas, its annual economic output was comparable to that of Billings, Montana. Life expectancy was a bleak forty-six years.[29]

Now that Afghanistan had been liberated, a central government established, and security maintained through ISAF, the second most daunting challenge for the Bush administration was to help rebuild the war-

---

[29] Bush, *Decision Points*, 174.

torn country. The term *rebuild* is an understatement considering the task ahead for all parties involved. The country's security forces—both police and military—were nonexistent. Afghanistan had a subsistence-level economy with no major trade or industrial production activities. Just like post-World War II Germany, Afghanistan's infrastructure lay in shambles with roads destroyed, bridges collapsed, canals dried up, and power grids torn apart. Government institutions were barely capable of providing minimal public services, and the education system for boys and girls lacked school supplies, textbooks, teachers, and classrooms. The challenge ahead was as formidable as it was in Europe after World War II, and it needed a strong commitment from the international community. Most importantly, it required a roadmap with concrete sets of deliverables backed by strong financial support by an international coalition led by the United States.

During one of their presidential election debates in 2000, then-governor of Texas George W. Bush and U.S. vice president Albert A. "Al" Gore Jr. debated the possibility of sending U.S. troops for nation-building efforts in any part of the world.[30] Bush came out strongly against this idea of using "our troops as nation builders." However, he later wrote in his memoir that

> *after 9/11, I changed my mind. Afghanistan was the ultimate nation-building mission. We had liberated the country from a primitive dictatorship, and we had a moral obligation to leave behind some-*

---

[30] "Presidential Candidates Debate," C-SPAN, 3 October 2000, 1:36:36 min.

thing better. We also had a strategic inter-
est in helping the Afghan people build a
free society. . . . A democratic Afghanistan
would be a hopeful alternative to the vi-
sion of the extremists.[31]

Bush's strategy for Afghanistan was threefold:

1. To liberate Afghanistan from the Taliban and fight the remnants of al-Qaeda in that country.

2. To help Afghanistan become a prosperous country in the region and serve as an example for other nations to see the strategic benefits of siding with the United States and the West. As part of this nation-building effort, the goal was also to strengthen the democratic institutions in Afghanistan and propagate the principles of democracy and market economy in the country.

3. To sell this dual-focused strategy of war and development in Afghanistan to those in Washington, DC.[32]

This strategy had to have a domestic front to answer the question of why the United States should spend so much money in Afghanistan. The answer to

---

[31] Bush, *Decision Points*, 174.

[32] For more on the Bush strategy, see Alex Roberto Hybel, "George W. Bush and the Afghan and Iraq Wars," in *US Foreign Policy Decision-Making from Kennedy to Obama: Responses to International Challenges* (New York: Palgrave Macmillan, 2014), https://doi .org/10.1057/9781137397690_5.

this question lies in the last pillar of Bush's strategy for Afghanistan: to fight the enemy who were thousands of kilometers ashore in Afghanistan and help build a prosperous democratic future for Afghans to prevent the country from becoming a breeding ground for terrorists who could strike the United States again.[33]

The Nation-Building Strategy, 2002–8

Following the initial U.S. airstrikes on the Taliban, which freed Afghanistan from their brutal regime and paved the way for the Northern Alliance to take control of the liberated cities, the Bush administration felt emboldened by this quick payoff. Twelve days after the first bombardments, American forces were on the ground in Afghanistan, and within 102 days of the 9/11 attacks, the United States had expelled the Taliban from the country and presumably dissipated al-Qaeda.[34] Afghanistan now had a new leader who was "forty-four years old with sharp features and a salt-and-pepper beard . . . [and] wore a shimmering green cape over his gray tunic, along with a pointed cap made of goatskin."[35] Most importantly, the United States and international forces were hailed as liberators and welcomed by the majority of Afghans—a reaction that few expected. According to an Asia Foundation survey

---

[33] George W. Bush, "President Bush Discusses Progress in Afghanistan, Global War on Terror" (speech, Mayflower Hotel, Washington, DC, 15 February 2007).

[34] Brian Neumann, Lisa Mundey, and Jon Mikolashek, *The United States Army in Afghanistan: Operation Enduring Freedom, March 2002–April 2005* (Fort Lesley J. McNair, Washington, DC: U.S. Army Center of Military History, 2002).

[35] Bush, *Decision Points*, 174.

from 2004, roughly two-thirds of Afghans surveyed were in favor of the United States (65 percent) and the U.S. military presence in Afghanistan (67 percent).[36] In the United States, support for going to war in Afghanistan was significantly positive as well, with 87 percent of Americans in support in October 2001.[37]

As a backdrop to this considerable support in the United States and abroad, the Bush administration took on the task of nation-building in Afghanistan. The following section focuses on these nation-building efforts and outlines the achievements, failures, and consequences of those interventions.

On 18 April 2002, seven months after the war in Afghanistan was announced, President Bush spoke before cadets at the Virginia Military Institute (VMI) and outlined America's role in a post-Taliban Afghanistan. Bush announced that military force alone could not bring "true peace" to Afghanistan unless the war-ravaged country reconstructed its roads, health care system, schools, and businesses, just as Europe and Japan did after World War II.[38]

In this speech, the president insisted that the United States was ready to lead an international effort in Afghanistan. He repeatedly invoked the name of U.S. Army general George C. Marshall, who graduated from VMI in 1901, served as U.S. president Harry S. Truman's secretary of state after World War II, and became

---

[36] *Afghanistan in 2004: A Survey of the Afghan People* (Kabul, Afghanistan: Asia Foundation, 2004).

[37] Chris Good, "When and Why Did Americans Turn against the War in Afghanistan?," *Atlantic*, 22 June 2011.

[38] George W. Bush, "President Outlines War Effort" (speech, Virginia Military Institute, Lexington, VA, 17 April 2002).

the chief architect of the European Recovery Program, more commonly known as the Marshall Plan.

"By helping to build an Afghanistan that is free from this evil and is a better place in which to live, we are working in the best traditions of George Marshall," Bush claimed. "Marshall knew that our military victory against enemies in World War II had to be followed by a moral victory that resulted in better lives for individual human beings."[39]

Indulging in some inspiration from Marshall, Bush's heart was in the right place for Afghanistan and the Afghan people. His vision, outlined in this speech, is what Afghanistan needed at that moment. It was the much-needed remedy for a war-torn nation. While the intentions of the U.S. government were noble, however, the question is whether the strategy panned out on the ground in Afghanistan as planned.

When the author's family returned to Afghanistan in 2002, his father took the author to the Ministry of Education in downtown Kabul. The route was lined with broken buildings and abandoned homes in a visibly deserted city (figure 14). The trip to the Ministry of Education was necessary to transfer the author's academic credentials from the Pakistani school, which he had previously attended, to the Afghan educational system.

---

[39] Bush elaborated further, "We know that true peace will only be achieved when we give the Afghan people the means to achieve their own aspirations. Peace will be achieved by helping Afghanistan develop its own stable government. Peace will be achieved by helping Afghanistan train and develop its own national army. And peace will be achieved through an education system for boys and girls which works." James Dao, "A Nation Challenged: The President; Bush Sets Role for U.S. in Afghan Rebuilding," *New York Times*, 18 April 2002.

Figure 14. Afghan children line up to enter the Rukhshana School in Kabul, Afghanistan

Source: official Department of Defense photo.

They entered the administrative building with all the necessary certificates and other supporting documents to prove the author's grade level in Pakistan, assuming that it would not be an issue to register in an Afghan school in the same grade. They were wrong. The man sitting behind the desk with a long dark beard and a turban refused to accept the papers. He insisted that the author be enrolled in a lower grade. The author's father realized that the Talib-like gentleman behind the desk was hinting at some sort of *shereni* (bribe). The author was dismissed to wait for his father outside. When he joined the author a few minutes later, he said that the gentleman had promised to sign the papers. The next day, the author's father handed him 500,000 Afghanis, which was equivalent to about $10 (USD), and was told to go back to the Ministry of Education and give the money to that gentleman discretely. He had the enrollment papers signed in his top drawer and requested the *shereni*. Though only one of thousands of similar personal stories, this story highlights the fact that corruption was endemic in Afghan institutions even in the early days of U.S. involvement. Even though it was 2002, the author had to bribe his way into a school, which should be every person's legitimate right.

On the first day in class, the students sat on a bare concrete floor because there were no desks or chairs. The classroom did have a roof and a blackboard with a small piece of chalk laying to the side. Due to a lack of teachers, one person would teach multiple subjects. After a few months, new desks and chairs were brought into the school. The building was renovated, classrooms painted, and new teachers hired, including female teachers. Newly published textbooks were brought in and distributed among the students. After the renovation was completed, a few government officials and foreigners came in to inaugurate the restoration of the school. The plaque near the entrance of the school bore the flag of the United States with a message stating this school renovation was made possible "with the assistance of the American people, through the United States Agency for International Development." Afghan schools were now a more suitable place for students to learn, thanks in large part to the funding from the American people.

Growing up as a refugee in Pakistan and living in post-Taliban Kabul, the author's textbooks, notebooks, and pens were all donated by the United States Agency for International Development (USAID), the United

Nations Children's Emergency Fund (UNICEF), and other development agencies.[40] As a result of those donations, Afghan children received a primitive-level education that, in the author's case, prepared him to later attend prestigious universities in the United States. Otherwise, most Afghan youth could not afford their books, dropped out of school, and later joined the ranks of the Taliban. The author received aid until 2004, when he was selected to participate in a one-year high school exchange program to the United States. Later, he returned for his undergraduate degree. The author is so passionate about development because he came out of the conflict zone successfully due to the help he received from aid agencies.

Before Bush outlined America's role in post-Taliban Afghanistan during his speech at VMI, Japan had offered to host a two-day international donor conference on reconstruction assistance for Afghanistan in January 2002. The goal was to raise money to rebuild a conflict-ravaged Afghanistan following the ejection of the Taliban. Representatives from nearly 60 countries and 20 international organizations participated in the conference, signaling strong international support.[41]

The broad consensus among all the donor countries was that Afghanistan needed financial support for reconstruction, and the newly appointed government of Hamid Karzai needed money to run the country. Donors were happy to contribute and did so generously.

[40] *Protecting Refugees: A Field Guide for NGOs* (New York: United Nations High Commissioner for Refugees, 1999).

[41] "Japan to Host Conference on Afghanistan in Early July," Japan International Cooperation Agency, May/June 2012.

They simply wanted to know how much money was needed. The UN presented a framework for funding and a needs assessment to donors at the Tokyo conference. According to the assessment conducted by the UN Development Programme, the Asian Development Bank, and the World Bank, the price tag for rebuilding Afghanistan was estimated at $15 billion (USD) during the next decade from 2003 to 2013. In the same vein, the UN presented a short-term program of about $1.33 billion to help with the immediate needs of the government and people of Afghanistan in the first year.[42]

At the end of the conference, the international donor community agreed on several key priorities for the reconstruction of Afghanistan. Education for girls, health care, infrastructure, agriculture, and reconstruction of the economic system were highlighted as five areas where the interim government and international donors needed to focus. Along with these priority areas, the Afghan Interim Authority led by Hamid Karzai also emphasized its commitment to transparency, efficiency, and accountability. The conference raised a significant amount of money. While some donor countries made multiyear commitments, others offered support in kind without specifying a monetary value. Overall, about $4.5 billion was raised for six years of aid.[43]

According to the USAID database, the United States spent $22.1 billion in Afghanistan between 2001

[42] "UN to Present Plans for Rebuilding Afghanistan at Donor Conference in Tokyo," UN News, 18 January 2002.

[43] "Co-chairs' Summary of Conclusions: The International Conference on Reconstruction Assistance to Afghanistan" (paper presented at International Conference on Reconstruction Assistance to Afghanistan, Tokyo, Japan, 21–22 January 2002).

Figure 15. Bush-era aid to Afghanistan, 2001–8, USD millions

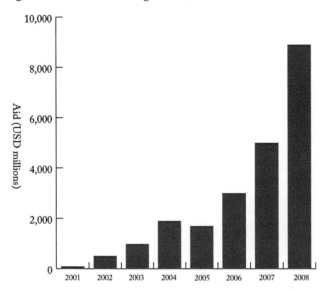

Source: "Foreign Aid Explorer," USAID, 2021.

and 2008.[44] The money was primarily appropriated for development purposes and not for military operations in the country. Afghanistan was the top aid recipient during this period, receiving on average $2.8 billion annually. No other country came close to receiving such large sums of aid money from the United States. As highlighted in the chart above, the amount of aid increased each year from $508 million in 2002 to about $8.9 billion in 2008, an increase of about 1,600 percent in seven years (figure 15).

The United States was not alone in this endeavor.

---

[44] "Foreign Aid Explorer," USAID, accessed 14 July 2021.

Figure 16. Aid contributions to Afghanistan, 2002–8, USD millions

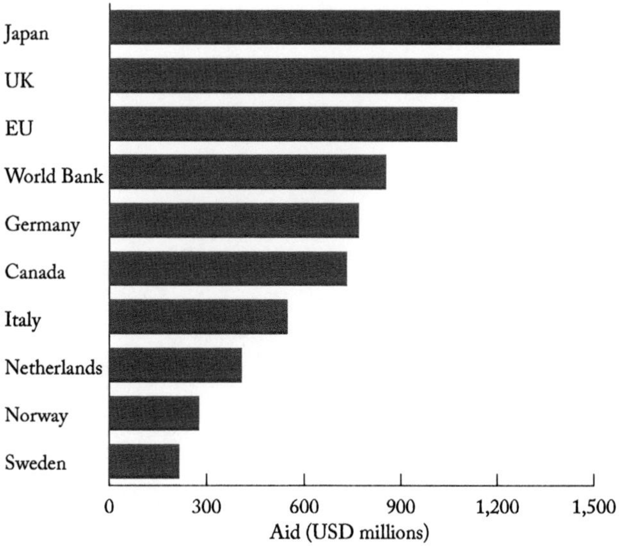

Source: "Foreign Aid Explorer," USAID, 2021.

More than 20 other nations contributed to the reconstruction efforts in Afghanistan as well. According to Oxfam International, the top 10 donor countries highlighted in figure 16 poured more than $7.5 billion into the country during 2002–8.[45]

Most of the $22.1 billion in aid that was provided by the United States between 2001 and 2008 (75.4 percent) was spent on programs related to the following three areas: Afghan security sector reform, infrastruc-

---

[45] Matt Waldman, *Falling Short: Aid Effectiveness in Afghanistan*, ACBAR Advocacy Series (Kabul, Afghanistan: Oxfam International, 2008).

Figure 17. Top sectors that received the most funding from Bush-era and USAID programs

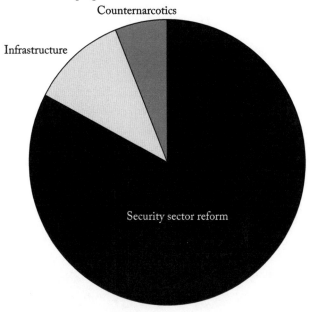

Source: "Foreign Aid Explorer," USAID, 2021.

ture, and counternarcotics. As highlighted in figure 17, Afghan security sector reform consumed more than $12.9 billion (62.5 percent); infrastructure, $1.7 billion (8.5 percent); and counternarcotics, $960 million (4.6 percent). The total price tag for these programs cost American taxpayers $15.5 billion.[46]

---

[46] "Foreign Aid Explorer."

CHAPTER THREE

Development Projects

The Security Sector Reform Program

At the Geneva Meeting on Afghan Security Sector in May 2002, the United States and other donor countries agreed to support the rebuilding of Afghanistan's security forces.[1] During the Soviet intervention of the 1980s, the Afghan National Police and Army had existed as organized forces based on the Soviet model. Officers were educated at a police academy, militarized, and well-equipped. During the Soviet-Afghan war and the period of Taliban rule that followed, law and order forces and the national defense army were disbanded. Guerrilla-like mujahideen forces and Taliban-like foot soldiers took charge of these institutions. There were no national civilian police or army forces in Afghanistan during this time.[2] In December 2001, following the defeat of the Taliban by U.S.-led Coalition forces, the Northern Alliance militia factions that had assisted U.S. forces in the fight exploited an opportunity to place their guerrilla force leaders in key positions at the Ministries of Interior Affairs and Defense. Most of these men had little to no professional training or experience.

---

[1] Mark Sedra, ed., *Confronting Afghanistan's Security Dilemma: Reforming the Security Sector*, Brief 28 (Bonn, Germany: Bonn International Center for Conversion, 2003).

[2] Andrew Wilder, *Cops or Robbers?: The Struggle to Reform the Afghan National Police*, Issues Paper Series (Kabul: Afghanistan Research and Evaluation Unit, 2007).

They had just come down from the Panjshir Mountains, where they had fought during the civil war and then held a stronghold against the Taliban.[3]

A daunting task for the international community, and most importantly for the United States, was to build an effective civilian police force and a national army bound by the rule of law and respect for human rights. The starting point was an estimated 50,000 untrained police, mostly unpaid or underpaid factional commanders and their militias, with little or no equipment or infrastructure.[4] At the Geneva conference, the United States took the lead to help build the Afghan National Army (ANA), and joined forces with Germany to train, equip, and advise the Afghan National Police (ANP).[5] In 2003, the U.S. Department of State established a police training center in Kabul to provide in-service training for Afghan police currently serving in the capital. The program began with three American instructors handling the training for a handful of trainees selected by the Ministry of Interior Affairs. It offered courses used at the Kosovo Police Service School, with an 8-week course in police skills, a 5-week course in literacy, and 15 days of active training. After the initial pilot run, the program greatly accelerated the num-

---

[3] Deedee Derksen, *The Politics of Disarmament and Rearmament in Afghanistan* (Washington, DC: U.S. Institute of Peace, 2015).

[4] T. X. Hammes, "Raising and Mentoring Security Forces in Afghanistan and Iraq," in Richard D. Hooker Jr. and Joseph J. Collins, eds., *Lessons Learned: Learning from the Long War* (Washington, DC: National Defense University Press, 2015).

[5] *Afghanistan Security: Efforts to Establish Army and Police Have Made Progress, but Future Plans Need to Be Better Defined*, GAO-05-575 (Washington, DC: Government Accountability Office, 2005).

ber of Afghan police who received training, with the total number reaching 71,147 by the end of 2007.[6]

In December 2006, a Joint report by the inspectors' general of the U.S. Departments of State and Defense found that U.S.-trained Afghan police were incapable of conducting routine law enforcement. The report also highlighted that Americans could not account for the equipment, vehicles, and weapons provided to the Afghan government as part of the training.[7] In the last few years, some of the police pickup trucks ended up in the Taliban's hands by attacking and controlling the police checkpoints. The report noted a suspicious number of "ghost police" who existed only on payroll lists. Police salaries were paid through the government by major donors, including the United States. The absence of reliable figures on police personnel numbers raised serious concerns that a significant amount of donor funds allocated for police salaries were being misappropriated. The salaries of these ghost police were pocketed either by the leadership at the Ministry of Interior Affairs or by militia commanders. While significant progress was made since then in reforming the payroll system for police salaries, such as developing individual salary payment (ISP) and electronic funds transfer (EFT) schemes, ghost police undoubtedly still existed.[8]

---

[6] Sedra, "Security Sector Reform and State Building in Afghanistan."

[7] *Interagency Assessment of Afghanistan Police Training and Readiness*, Department of State Report No. ISP-IQO-07-07, Department of Defense Report No. IE-2007-001 (Washington, DC: Inspectors General, U.S. Department of State and U.S. Department of Defense, 2006).

[8] *Interagency Assessment of Afghanistan Police Training and Readiness.*

According to a report by the Special Inspector General for Afghanistan Reconstruction (SIGAR), the Pentagon wasted more than $28 million on Afghan Army camouflage.[9] Most of Afghanistan's terrain is desert, and the ANA needed a uniform that would resemble the landscape in its area of operations. However, in this case, the Department of Defense agreed to purchase a camouflage pattern that replicated lush forests and paid $28 million for the procurement of such a uniform. According to the report, the Afghan minister of defense, Abdul Rahim Wardak, picked the pattern based on his fashion preference while browsing the internet, not based on advice from experts. "That was a dumb decision," said John F. Sopko, the special inspector general. "It's the totally wrong pattern for a country like Afghanistan. We are in Afghanistan; 98 percent of it is desert, so you would assume you want something that blended with the desert."[10] The report noted that altering the army's uniform could have saved the United States between $68.6 and $72.2 million over 10 years.[11]

The real question is this: What outcome was achieved by pouring such a massive amount of money during a period of six years—nearly $13 billion—into the security sector of Afghanistan? The answer is simple: very little progress was achieved. Corruption still ran rampant across the security sector in both the ANP and ANA. People did not feel safe, and the ANA strug-

---

[9] *ANA Proprietary Camouflaged Uniforms*, SIGAR-17-48-SP (Arlington, VA: Special Inspector General for Afghanistan Reconstruction, 2017).

[10] Megan Specia, "'A Dumb Decision:' U.S. Said to Waste $28 Million on Afghan Army Camouflage," *New York Times*, 21 June 2017.

[11] *ANA Proprietary Camouflaged Uniforms*.

gled to survive the barrage of attacks from the Taliban. The *San Francisco Chronicle* ran a story on 28 May 2007 that profiled a truck driver named Abad Khan, describing how "Afghan truck drivers quiver from lawlessness, not [the] Taliban."[12] Khan is quoted as saying, "We pay all our bribes to criminals, and they are criminals who wear police uniforms." These truck drivers were the primary transporters of goods and fuel to foreign forces in the country. They were often stopped by police on main highways and asked for bribes ranging from $1 to $60 (USD). In some instances, fuel tankers were pulled over so police officers could fill up their cars. Another truck driver said, "Forget about the Taliban. Our biggest problems are with the police."[13]

In 2018, the Asia Foundation's annual survey polled 6,263 people across all 34 provinces in Afghanistan. The respondents were all asked about their main causes for concern, with the majority (36 percent) citing security as the biggest challenge facing Afghanistan, more so than economic issues and unemployment.[14] In the same survey, the percentage of people who feared for their personal well-being and security had reached its highest level since 2002, with 38 percent of the respondents saying they often feared for their safety. In addition, 49 percent of the respondents said they had some fear encountering officers of the ANP.[15] Unfortunately, Af-

---

[12] Chris Sands, "Afghan Truck Drivers Quiver from Lawlessness, Not Taliban," *San Francisco (CA) Chronicle*, 28 May 2007.

[13] Sands, "Afghan Truck Drivers Quiver from Lawlessness, not Taliban."

[14] *Afghanistan in 2008: A Survey of the Afghan People* (Kabul, Afghanistan: Asia Foundation, 2008).

[15] *Afghanistan in 2008*, 32.

ghans had created very little confidence in their security forces, despite the massive investment by the United States and various other donor countries.

Infrastructure

Infrastructure is the bedrock of any country, and post-Taliban Afghanistan was in dire need of reconstructing its roads, bridges, schools, and hospitals that had been destroyed in the previous four decades. One of the first major projects that the United States embarked on following the removal of the Taliban was the reconstruction of the Kabul-Kandahar Highway. In 2003, the U.S. ambassador to Afghanistan Zalmay M. Khalilzad stood with President Hamid Karzai at a ribbon-cutting ceremony inaugurating the completion of phase I (482 kilometers) of the highway (figure 18). This project was a massive undertaking by the United States to show the people of Afghanistan and the wider region that partnering with the United States pays great dividends. In his remarks at the opening ceremony, Khalilzad said, "This is a good day. We are standing—literally—on the road to Afghanistan's future. It is a future of national unity. It is a future of prosperity. It is a future of peace."[16]

Between 1979 and 1989, the Soviet Union had financed a slew of road projects in Afghanistan, laying the groundwork for much of the country's road system. This included the system for the Ring Road, which divides Kandahar and the capital city of Kabul. However, four decades of war largely destroyed the infrastructure

---

[16] Zalmay Khalilzad, "Dedication Ceremony for the Phase I Completion, Kabul-Kandahar Highway" (speech, Durrani, Afghanistan, 16 December 2003).

Figure 18. Military convoys patrol the new highway, sharing the road with local traffic

Source: official U.S. Air Force photo.

across the country, starting with the Soviet invasion in the 1980s and followed closely by civil wars and the Taliban's rise. Much of the Ring Road was reduced to a dirt track during the Taliban rule in the late 1990s, despite modest road improvements. The length of the wars and lack of infrastructure led to considerable deterioration of roads, bridges, and tunnels. According to a 1994 road condition survey, only 17 percent of the roads were assessed to be in good condition. The average pace on the Kabul-Kandahar road was approximately 24 kilometers per hour, and the 482-kilometer journey from Kabul to Kandahar took roughly 20 hours.[17]

The United States Agency for International Development (USAID) estimates that Afghanistan had about 50 kilometers of paved roads after the Taliban were deposed.[18] It conducted an Afghanistan civil infrastructure assessment and delivered a final report to the Afghan government, concluding that the restoration of important roadways, notably the Ring Road, was a top priority for Afghanistan's infrastructure. In 2001, the Asian Development Bank (ADB) conducted a road state survey and presented a report to the board of directors, stating that Afghanistan's road infrastructure was in desperate need of repair because "damaged highways have become bottlenecks to the passage of people and goods."[19] The country's economy would remain at a standstill without roads, since people would find it difficult to travel from one location to another and local products would be late to market. Based on these studies and proposals from USAID and ADB,

---

[17] *Comprehensive Needs Assessment for Reconstruction in the Transport Sector–Afghanistan* (Mandaluyong, Philippines: Asian Development Bank, 2002).

[18] U.S. Congress, House of Representatives, Committee on Appropriations, Subcommittee on Foreign Operations, Export Financing, and Related Programs, USAID Accomplishments in Afghanistan, 109th Cong., 1st Sess. (11 September 2006).

[19] *Comprehensive Needs Assessment for Reconstruction in the Transport Sector–Afghanistan.*

the Afghan government and international partners suggested a road network for Afghanistan, which they aimed to complete by 2015.[20] The proposed network prioritized the country's major roadways connecting Kabul to major cities including Kandahar, Mazari Sharif, and Herat.

The first significant Ring Road project was sponsored by USAID in 2002. The Kabul-Kandahar Highway connects the two cities that bear its name. It is one of the country's most significant roadways, spanning 482 kilometers to the south and connecting the nation. The Bush administration initially rejected the Afghan government's plan to restore the route, claiming that USAID had never completed road repair projects in post-conflict areas. However, given the significance of this route and its influence on Afghan life, USAID hired the Louis Berger Group (LBG) to rebuild the Kabul-Kandahar road as part of a large infrastructure program.[21]

By early 2003, the roadway had become a major U.S. objective, and USAID was under constant pressure from Washington to show progress. Despite deaths, attacks, helicopter accidents, and supply difficulties, LBG engineers and personnel remained dedicated to the deadline. LBG completed phase one of the project and turned it over to the Afghan government at the end of 2003. The renovation of this route, which was originally

---

[20] *Afghanistan Reconstruction: Progress Made in Constructing Roads, but Assessments for Determining Impact and a Sustainable Maintenance Program Are Needed*, Report No. GAO-08-689 (Washington, DC: Government Accountability Office, 2008), 5.

[21] *Afghanistan Reconstruction.*

projected to cost $162 million, ended up costing $311 million. In essence, each kilometer of road repair cost the U.S. taxpayers around $1 million.[22]

The Japan International Cooperation Agency (JICA) sponsored another section of the Kabul-Kandahar route, called Section G, for $29 million (USD), covering roughly 50 kilometers of road. They also used LBG to complete the job. LBG subcontracted with Indian and South African companies, who in turn subcontracted with local Afghan businesses, who found further subcontractors in both situations.[23]

Final reports and donor evaluations show the positive impact of the Kabul-Kandahar project. The highway enhanced efficiency by facilitating movement and transit, and it contributed to a considerable increase in business activities and income for people living within its zone of impact (an area 15 kilometers wide on either side of the road). Farmers are now able to expand their market outside local towns and boost their profits, as transportation costs have decreased.[24]

In addition to its economic effects, the road had several positive social consequences. Many social services, including schools and medical facilities, opened up throughout the zone of influence. Villagers could now take their ill or injured to provincial capitals or Kabul for better care. Because of the increasing number of

---

[22] *Afghanistan: U.S.- and Internationally-Funded Roads (GAO-09-626SP), an E-supplement to GAO-09-473SP* (Washington, DC: Government Accountability Office, 2009).

[23] *Afghanistan: U.S.- and Internationally-Funded Roads.*

[24] Mafizul Islam, *Roads Socio-Economic Impact Assessment: Kabul–Kandahar Road* (Kabul: USAID Afghanistan, 2008), 1.

schools and greater access to transportation, more female students were now able to attend school.[25]

In terms of sustainability, none of the donor organizations, including USAID, took substantial measures to ensure the road's long-term maintenance.
Rather, they delegated that authority to the Afghan
government. However, the government failed to fulfill
its responsibilities due to a variety of issues, including
a lack of human and financial resources. Because of
these flaws, the government was unable to collect fees
for the maintenance of the newly constructed road.
The Kabul-Kandahar Highway is now in disrepair,
with significant potholes caused by both wear and tear
and roadside explosives in unstable regions. According
to the World Bank, 85 percent of the road is in "poor
condition, and the majority cannot be utilized by mo-
tor vehicles."[26] Figure 19 depicts what remains of the
multimillion-dollar road project.

The road maintenance process was also hampered
by a lack of capability in the private sector. Donors advised the Afghan Ministry of Public Works to include
the private sector in road maintenance efforts. However,
when the government asked for bids to maintain the
Kabul-Kandahar road in 2006, it did not get a single
proposal. As a result, the European Commission and
USAID agreed to pay for temporary upkeep. The World

[25] Z. Wu et al., *Afghanistan: Andkhoy-Qaisar Road Project*, Completion Report No. 37075 (Mandaluyong, Philippines: Asian Development Bank, 2010), 3.

[26] Tom A. Peter, "Paved Roads a Positive Legacy of Afghan War. But
Who Fixes Potholes?," *Christian Science Monitor*, 2 February 2015.

Figure 19. ADB provided $30 million for reconstruction of Kabul-Kandahar Highway that now lies in ruin

Source: Ariana News, Kabul, Afghanistan.

Bank also stated that it would support a $72 million (USD) yearly maintenance program.[27]

The ultimate goal driving this massive post-conflict road rebuilding effort was to keep Afghanistan from de-

---

[27] *Proposed Grant for an Afghanistan Rural Access Project*, No. 69508-AF (Washington, DC: World Bank, 2012).

volving into a failed state and posing a threat to world security. Former U.S. military commander and ambassador to Afghanistan Karl W. Eikenberry famously remarked, "Where the road stops, the Taliban begins."[28] Was his assertion true?

A *New York Times* story from 2007 offered a bleak image of the security condition on the Kabul-Kandahar Highway, stating that it was still plagued with danger, extortion, and betrayal. Police corruption and rebel attacks continued to frighten the populace, and traveling on portions of the route was dangerous at best. The Taliban used to conduct attacks on the road, and criminal activity such as robberies and extortion were widespread. Armed groups set up roadblocks and chased their victims on motorcycles and trucks.[29]

While donor agency reports minimized the danger along this route, publications such as *The New York Times*, *The Washington Post*, and *The Telegraph* have widely reported on the road's instability since the project's launch. According to *The Telegraph*, "the Kabul–Kandahar Route was built at great expenditure as a symbol of achievement for the new Afghanistan, but instead the . . . road has become a highway of death that exposes what has gone wrong." The Taliban, according to the report, were well aware of the significance of the road, and insurgents continued to launch assaults along the route. The statistics for road violence are grim, with 190 bomb attacks and 284 shootings in 2018, roughly

---

[28] Donald P. Wright, *A Different Kind of War: The United States Army in Operation Enduring Freedom* (Fort Leavenworth, KS: Combat Studies Institute Press, U.S. Army Combined Arms Center, 2010).
[29] C. J. Chivers, "Trouble on a Vital Road in Afghanistan," *New York Times*, 3 December 2007.

one for every kilometer of road. The Kabul-Kandahar Highway has been a hot spot for rebel strikes and criminal activity for a number of reasons, including that corruption permeates not just the Afghan government but also development programs. Afghanistan's contractual processes were riddled with loopholes that allowed Afghan government officials, construction companies, and donor agency officials to misappropriate cash.[30]

After a whistleblower revealed that the contractor had overbilled the U.S. government and bribed the Taliban to defend the road project, federal authorities punished LBG with the largest punitive assessment in a wartime contracting case in November 2012. LBG paid criminal fines of $18.7 million and civil penalties of $50.6 million. Due to loopholes, funding ended up in the hands of the Taliban, and contract procedures—or lack thereof—permitted LBG to engage an Indian subcontractor, as a joint venture of two other businesses, to conduct the work. The Indian firm then subcontracted the project to Afghan warlords who did not even have a registered business. Afghan subcontractors paid the Taliban millions of dollars to provide security and ensure that the project would not be attacked.[31]

These massive road developments bolstered the influence of warlords and the Taliban. Now that development is complete, warlords who profited financially from the project have greater power along the road. Their followers frequently dress up as police officers and

[30] Ben Framer, "Kabul-Kandahar Highway Is a Symbol of What's Gone Wrong in Afghanistan," *Telegraph*, 9 September 2012.

[31] James Risen, "Costly Afghanistan Road Project Is Marred by Unsavory Alliances," *New York Times*, 1 May 2011.

set up roadblocks. "They pose as Afghan National Police because they can stop someone with a Kalashnikov [AK-47] and half a uniform," stated U.S. Army captain Matthew T. Hagerman. These armed people robbed travelers and abducted humanitarian workers. They also gave the Taliban the ability to plant improvised explosive devices (IEDs) and struck North Atlantic Treaty Organization (NATO) supply convoys. In the end, these acts fed instability and allowed them to continue their illegal operations.[32]

Opium trafficking is the second most critical security risk along the Kabul-Kandahar Highway. According to the UN, "after 12 years of [the] US-led war in Afghanistan, the nation remains the world's largest opium source, accounting for 90% of global supply."[33] While the Kabul-Kandahar road reconstruction has benefited the populations along the route, it has also presented a challenge to opium traffickers, especially given that 70 percent of narcotics trafficking occurs along major highways. There were fewer police checkpoints when the route was only a dirt track, allowing drug dealers to transport opium without being stopped by authorities. Although drug dealers continue to scare law enforcement by attacking checkpoints, a larger police presence became possible now that the road conditions had improved. However, local government officials continued to accept bribes and backed the traffickers in certain situations. While donor organizations evaluated the

---

[32] Carlotta Gall, "Afghanistan's Kabul-Kandahar Highway: A Lifeline Plagued with Insurgents," *New York Times*, 13 August 2008.
[33] Tom A. Peter, "Afghanistan Still World's Top Opium Supplier, Despite 10 Years of US-led War," *Christian Science Monitor*, 11 October 2011.

impact of their projects on the economic well-being of communities along the route, they either failed to recognize or overlooked the likelihood of smugglers and illicit drug traffickers misusing the road.[34]

The project designers' failure to comprehend local Afghan social structures is the final and most crucial element contributing to an increase in violence along the route. Afghanistan is a tribal culture, with local leaders wielding considerably more power in rural regions than the central government. According to the World Bank, project execution in a conflict-affected setting like Afghanistan requires a detailed grasp of the local social structure, as well as the capacity to engage with community leaders to ensure project site access and security. A project like this was intended to create jobs in rural areas while also giving local leaders a say in the design and implementation. The road project was instead outsourced to international firms. Local Afghan elders were generally ignored while certain local contractors or warlords were employed to undertake a section of the project. They were mostly absent from the decision-making and execution phases. The projects did not employ locals, instead bringing Indian, Turkish, and Chinese workers in from other countries. Because they were cut out of the process, local residents did not feel compelled to support the initiative.[35]

While $15.5 billion—almost 75.4 percent—of the overall U.S. aid package to Afghanistan during 2002–8 was allocated to the security sector reform, infrastruc-

---

[34] *Monitoring of Drug Flows in Afghanistan* (Kabul: Afghanistan: United Nations Office on Drugs and Crime, 2007).
[35] *Proposed Grant for an Afghanistan Rural Access Project.*

Figure 20. Sectors receiving the least funding from U.S. aid programs, 2002–8

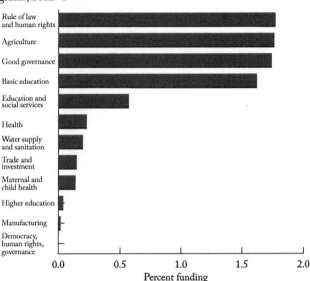

Source: "Foreign Aid Explorer," USAID, 2021.

ture, and counternarcotics programs, the following sectors received only a small fraction—just 8 percent—of the total aid (figure 20).[36]

The rule of law and human rights program and the agriculture program each received about $362 million over six years. Basic education programs were awarded $364 million, while the health sector received about $46 million. Most importantly, maternal and child health, higher education, and trade investment programs combined only received about $69 million from 2002 to 2008. The most shocking figure shows that the last sec-

---

[36] "Foreign Aid Explorer," USAID Data, accessed 16 July 2021.

tor—democracy, human rights, and governance—only received about $5,000 in six years.[37]

It is important to highlight these figures and compare them with the top three sectors: security, infrastructure, and counternarcotics. While the latter sectors absorbed massive amounts of U.S. aid in the first six years of the war and yielded very few results, investing in the former sectors such as agriculture, basic education, and maternal health are critical for any country but extremely vital for a country like Afghanistan.[38] It is a matter of life and death for a mother giving birth to a child in a hospital with no trained nurses or, even worse, with no hospital or clinic at all. While infrastructure paves the way for economic development, investment in quality education enlightens an entire generation so they cannot be easily targeted by extremists. Eradicating narcotics is a good idea, but investing in farmers and providing them with an alternative crop provides them the means to feed themselves for ages.

The reality is that when it came to investing their hard-earned taxpayer money in Afghanistan, donor nations got all of their priorities wrong. The Afghan government and donor nations never agreed on a set of long-term initiatives for Afghanistan's economic growth. As a staffer at the Policy Department of the Ministry of Finance in Afghanistan between 2016 and 2018, the author was assigned to help align the National Priority Programs (NPP) of the Afghan government

---

[37] "Foreign Aid Explorer."
[38] "Foreign Aid Explorer."

with major donors' wish lists.[39] That portfolio included the infrastructure NPP, the urban development NPP, and the human capital development program. Overall, the government had 10 priority areas where they wanted international donors to invest. However, the issue of mismatched priorities between the Afghan government and international donors made it difficult to streamline funding for much-needed sectors. Unfortunately, the issue of donor fragmentation existed from the early days of this war.[40]

It was not until 2005 that the Afghan government developed a strategy paper called the *Afghanistan National Development Strategy: An Interim Strategy for Security, Governance, Economic Growth & Poverty Reduction*. It was a 300-page document that outlined the government's vision for economic development and its political and security priorities. While the gesture was genuine, most of the priorities outlined in the document were vague, unrealistic, and mere tag lines for donors at the London Conference for Afghanistan in 2006.[41] The document envisioned "high rates of sustainable and eq-

---

[39] *National Priority Programs* (NPP) refer to a set of 22 priority programs announced at the Kabul Conference in 2010. While the *Afghanistan National Development Strategy* (ANDS) provides an overall strategy, the NPP represent a prioritization and further focusing of the ANDS, including specific deliverables and costs. In addition, there are more than 10 NPP that existed before and continue to operate, such as the National Solidarity Program. The new NPPs are currently being finalized and will significantly advance the ability of government to direct resources into areas that will have the greatest national impact.

[40] "National Priority Programs," Office of the Deputy Minister for Policy, Ministry of Finance, Islamic Republic of Afghanistan, 2016.

[41] "The London Conference and the Afghanistan Compact," Department of State, 31 January 2006.

uitable economic growth [by 2020] ... to build a liberal market economy in which all Afghans can participate productively without engaging in production or trafficking of narcotics or other criminal activities."[42] The paper also outlined access to primary education for all children in the country who would attend secondary school. The government committed itself to "fight corruption [and] uphold justice and the rule of law."[43] What came out of the London Conference for Afghanistan was a list of 43 benchmarks and a timeline agreed on by all the donors. The deadline for achieving the benchmarks was the end of 2010, a four-year time frame.[44]

Under the public administration reform benchmark, the Afghan government was tasked with "ensur[ing] a fiscally sustainable public administration" by the end of 2010. Moreover, "a clear and transparent national appointments mechanism will be established within 6 months, applied within 12 months and fully implemented within 24 months for all senior level appointments to the central government and the judiciary, as well as for provincial governors, chiefs of police, district administrators and provincial heads of securi-

---

[42] *Afghanistan National Development Strategy: An Interim Strategy for Security, Governance, Economic Growth & Poverty Reduction,* vol. 1 (Kabul: Islamic Republic of Afghanistan, 2005), 16. This report has since been updated; see *Afghanistan National Development Strategy, 1387–1391 (2008–2013): A Strategy for Security, Governance, Economic Growth & Poverty Reduction* (Kabul: Islamic Republic of Afghanistan, 2010).

[43] *Afghanistan National Development Strategy,* 16.

[44] *Building on Success: The London Conference on Afghanistan—The Afghanistan Compact* (Brussels, Belgium: North Atlantic Treaty Organization, 2006), hereafter *The Afghanistan Compact.*

ty."[45] This benchmark was never achieved. Government appointments were mostly carried out at the discretion of the minister. Young Afghans newly graduated from colleges around the country and abroad could not find work because they did not know senior officials in the government who could vouch for them or hire them outright. During the Ghani administration, the Independent Administrative Reform and Civil Service Commission attempted a merit-based hiring process for all government appointments, but it did not make much progress. They could not vet candidates without external influence from warlords, senior government officials, or bribes.[46]

In addition, public administration is not yet fiscally sustainable. Until the day the previous government collapsed, donors funded a significant portion of Afghan government employees' monthly salary. The Afghan government did not have the means to pay its civilian staff.[47]

Another benchmark was to provide electricity to at least 65 percent of households and 90 percent of nonresidential establishments in major urban areas by the end of 2010.[48] However, by the end of 2009, Professor Abdul Rahman Ashraf, senior advisor to President Karzai, reported the following at an international conference on the Afghan energy sector:

---

[45] *The Afghanistan Compact*, 7.

[46] "Reforms in Review Part 5: Reforming the Civil Service Commission and Public Sector," Office of the Deputy Minister for Policy, Ministry of Finance, 2018.

[47] Kay Johnson, "Cash-poor Afghanistan Will Delay Paying Civil Servants: Finance Ministry Official," Reuters, 27 September 2014.

[48] *The Afghanistan Compact*.

- Only 10–15 percent of the Afghan population have access to electricity, one of the lowest figures in the world.
- About 3 percent of households (or 650,000) are connected to the national grid, mostly in large cities such as Kabul, Mazari Sharif, Herat, Kandahar, Jalalabad, etc.
- Approximately 340,000 customers are connected to the public power grid, 182,000 of which are in Kabul.
- The per-person total energy consumption is less than 25 kilowatt-hours (kWh) each year, compared to India (520 kWh), Germany (6,200 kWh), and the world average (3,060 kWh).
- Afghanistan sees a continuously rising energy demand, but most power stations are 40 years old and need to be rehabilitated.
- About 85 percent of the energy demand is covered by traditional biomass (e.g., wood and dung).[49]

In the education sector, primary and secondary education were considered a higher priority. The government of Afghanistan intended to achieve at least 60–70

---

[49] This list was adapted from Abdul Rahman, "Energy Sector Afghanistan: Importance of Renewable Energy for Afghanistan—Renewable Energy for Sustainable Development" (presentation, International Conference on Renewable Energy in Central Asia: Creating Economic Sustainability to Solve Socio-Economic Challenges, Dushanbe, Tajikistan, 10–11 November 2009).

percent net enrollment of boys and girls in primary school by the end of 2010. While the enrollment quota of 70 percent was achieved in major cities, the United Nations Children's Emergency Fund (UNICEF) reported in 2018 that an estimated 3.7 million children were not in school, including 60 percent of the girls in the entire country.[50] Low female enrollment was partly due to the lack of female teachers, the report noted, especially in rural areas. Only 16 percent of schools were girls-only and many of them lacked proper sanitation facilities, which further hindered attendance.[51]

Under the poverty-reduction benchmark, the government had promised to decrease the proportion of people living on less than $1 a day (USD) by 3 percent per year and a total reduction of 9 percent by the end of 2010. The percentage of people living below the poverty line has since increased by 9 percent, according to a recent United Nations Development Programme human development report (figure 21).[52]

Financial management was yet another indicator for the Afghan government to achieve by the end of 2010. At the donor's conference in London, the government had promised to establish a transparent financial management system that meets the International Monetary Fund's (IMF) requirements and all other international standards.[53] In turn, the donors would make more effort

[50] "Education: Providing Quality Education for All," UNICEF, 2018.

[51] "Education."

[52] *Afghanistan Human Development Report 2020: Pitfalls and Promise* (Kabul: UNDP Afghanistan Country Office, 2020).

[53] "The IMF at a Glance," International Monetary Fund, 3 March 2021.

Figure 21. Percentage of the Afghan population living below the poverty line, 2000–18

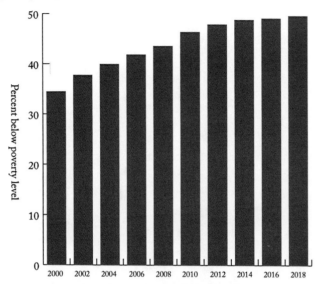

Source: *Afghanistan Human Development Report 2020.*

to channel a higher percentage of their financial support through the Afghan budget. In other words, donors will give their aid dollars directly to the Afghan government to use on projects rather than donors having to support their desired programs directly. When the author worked at the Ministry of Finance, the minister's priority was financial management, and the country had not been successful on this front even by the time the author departed in 2018. As a result, the donors never trusted the government to spend their aid money, and they slowly walked back their promise of spending more through the Afghan government budget. Recently, the

Figure 22. Foreign aid and domestic revenue

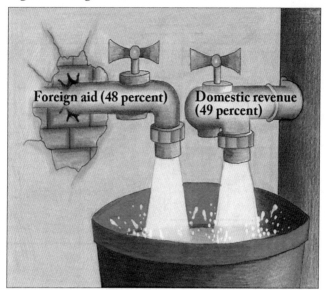

Source: "1400 National Budget Document," Ministry of Finance, Islamic Republic of Afghanistan, adapted by MCUP.

Ministry of Finance published its 2020 budget. According to this document, international donors spent 34.61 percent of their overall assistance aid through the Afghan government national budget. The remaining 65.4 percent remained at the discretion of the donors, and the Afghan government had very little say in it.[54]

Figure 22, which comes from the 2020 Afghan government budget proposal, highlights the fact that 48 percent of the national budget was comprised of foreign

[54] "1400 National Budget Document," Ministry of Finance, Islamic Republic of Afghanistan, 9 March 2021.

aid and 49 percent of domestic revenue. Sadly, this image further demonstrates that in the 20 years since the 9/11 attacks and the U.S. intervention in Afghanistan, almost one-half of the Afghan national budget still came from donor countries. There was no bigger threat to Afghanistan and what Afghans had achieved in the last two decades with the help from the United States than aid dependency. This type of monetary reliance was perpetual and never resulted in long-term economic development in the country.[55]

Until the day the Afghan government collapsed in August 2021, none of the aforementioned goals outlined at the 2006 London donor conference had been fully achieved. The Afghan economy was still in shambles, illicit drug trafficking was widespread, and a large portion of school-age children were unable to attend school due to a variety of issues including insecurity and a lack of school buildings, supplies, and trained teachers. Corruption was endemic and omnipresent in the government, and the rule of law was marred by bribery, intimidation, and subjugation of the underprivileged.

---

[55] The citizens budget can be found at "1400 National Budget Document."

CHAPTER FOUR

The Obama Doctrine

The Counterinsurgency Strategy

On 27 March 2009, the newly elected president of the United States, Barack H. Obama, stood before the American people and announced his strategy for the war in Afghanistan and Pakistan. He was now the second U.S. president to preside over this prolonged war, and he believed he had a remedy for the stalemate in Afghanistan. Having campaigned on a platform that the United States needed to refocus its fight in Afghanistan, the American people were already somewhat familiar with Obama's stance on the war. He insisted on withdrawing U.S. combat troops from Iraq on a fixed timeline and instead ramping up the American military effort in Afghanistan.[1] Now that he was president, it was time to act, and he did so by announcing his approach to the war.

Obama focused his strategy on a fundamental issue: questioning Pakistan's role in the war in Afghanistan. The war had intensified across Afghanistan, and 2008 represented the deadliest year there for American troops. In his speech, Obama put forth the central question: "What is our purpose in Afghanistan? After so many years, [we] ask, why do our men and women still fight and die there? And [we] deserve a straightforward

---

[1] Catherine Dale, *Operation Iraqi Freedom: Strategies, Approaches, Results, and Issues for Congress* (Washington, DC: Congressional Research Service, 2008).

answer."[2] He went on to highlight his goal for the war, which was to "disrupt, dismantle and defeat al Qaeda in Pakistan and Afghanistan, and to prevent their return to either country in the future."[3] Furthermore, he noted that after the Iraq War began in 2003, Afghanistan had been denied the necessary resources to succeed. The president committed to providing those resources, including financial assistance to the government of Afghanistan, to accomplish the aforementioned goals.[4]

In his first major military decision as commander in chief of the U.S. armed forces, Obama ordered the deployment of 17,000 troops to Afghanistan in February 2009.[5] Later that spring, he sent 4,000 additional troops to train Afghan security forces and accelerate the efforts to build the Afghan National Army (ANA).[6] Obama substantially increased the U.S. presence in Afghanistan during his first two years in office; total numbers of military personnel jumped from a little more than 30,000 in 2009 to more than 100,000 in 2011. A new commander, U.S. Army general Stanley A. McChrystal, was ordered to lead the war effort.[7]

On the economic development front, Obama un-

---

[2] Barack H. Obama, "Remarks by the President on a New Strategy for Afghanistan and Pakistan," White House, 27 March 2009, hereafter Obama remarks.

[3] Obama remarks.

[4] Obama remarks.

[5] Andrew Gray, "Obama Orders 17,000 U.S. Troops to Afghanistan," Reuters, 17 February 2009.

[6] Exploring Three Strategies for Afghanistan: Hearing Before the Committee on Foreign Relations, 111th Cong., 1st Sess. (16 September 2009).

[7] Danielle Kurtzleben, "How the U.S. Troop Levels in Afghanistan Have Changed under Obama," NPR, 6 July 2016.

derscored the fact that "our efforts will fail in Afghanistan and Pakistan if we don't invest in their future."[8] The American mission in Afghanistan had always been a military one, but with it also came humanitarian assistance in the form of grants and development aid through the United States Agency for International Development (USAID). The Obama administration wanted to couple U.S. military might with financial support to win the hearts and minds of the population. As a result of this massive surge in troops and financial support to the government of Afghanistan, U.S. development assistance through USAID peaked during 2011 and 2012, reaching about $13 billion (figure 23).[9]

The author was a sophomore at a small liberal arts college called St. Lawrence University, located in a remote area of upstate New York that was known for its long, cold winters and Sergi's Italian Pizzeria, when Obama became the 44th president of the United States. It was the author's first time witnessing American democracy firsthand, and he had closely followed all the presidential debates between Obama and his election opponent, John S. McCain III. Everyone openly shared their political views via various student clubs on campus—liberals, conservatives, and everything between.

Observing the election of the first African American president of the United States was monumental for this young foreign-exchange student, who was watching the election-day coverage live in the college's student center with hundreds of other students.

---

[8] Obama remarks.
[9] "Foreign Aid Explorer," USAID, 2021.

Figure 23. U.S. aid to Afghanistan, 2001–19, USD millions

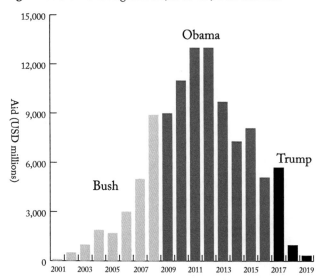

Source: "Foreign Aid Explorer," USAID, 2021.

As the final tally came in, a big cheer erupted in the back of the room when Obama was announced the winner. Students ran out of the student center, making their way to the quad to cheer, dance, and set off firecrackers until late in the evening. The jubilation for this foreign student was immense because of the ties between Afghanistan and the United States. Knowing how dependent Afghanistan was on the United States, Obama's election meant peace and prosperity for the author's home country.

Not long after that joyful night, an uncle who lived in Boston called one early winter morning when the author was in class, asking to meet him in an hour near the chapel. He said that he was going to Canada to visit a friend and stopped by on this way north. He asked the author to join him for breakfast at the university inn, where he had stayed the night before. As soon as they entered the uncle's room, he locked the door and uttered words the author would never forget: "Your father passed away." The uncle then called the author's brother in Kabul, who tried to calm the author down and talk him through what had happed and how their father died. He assured the author that the burial and all other rituals had taken place with great dignity, and that their father was now in a better place. The author had hoped to return to Afghanistan after receiving his economics degree and discuss so many topics with his father, who had also been an economist. He dreamed of sharing his study abroad experience and showing his father how much he had learned in the United States. All those aspirations were gone.

The author's father had fallen victim to the crippled healthcare system in Afghanistan. When the author was growing up, his father always complained about intestinal pain. He was told repeatedly by doctors that he had excess acid in his digestive system, which caused severe pain in his stomach. He was prescribed dozens of medications, and he took them all, but none of them made a significant difference. He had no other underlying health issues and was seemingly as healthy as a 20-year-old. He was told by a prominent doctor in Kabul that removing his gallbladder might help with his abdominal pain.

After a week of deliberation, he decided to take

the doctor's advice and agreed to undergo the surgical procedure. According to the medical department at the University of California, San Francisco, the removal of the gallbladder is considered a minimally invasive surgery.[10] Unlike open surgery, the number of cuts is limited in size and scope. The patient recovers more quickly and spends less time in the hospital. However, this is not the case in Afghanistan. Removing a gallbladder can cost your life. The author's father died about eight hours after the surgery due to severe internal bleeding. The author's brother said that he came out of the surgery fine and was speaking to him during that time until he appeared to doze off. When his brother ran out to find a nurse at the hospital, no one was there. The internal bleeding was so serious that it took the father's life within an hour. Had he been attended to at the right time, would that have made a difference? Who dropped the ball: the doctor or the nurse? These questions remain troubling even 11 years later.

The moral of this story is that the health sector in Afghanistan remains underdeveloped, even today. Hundreds of people queue up in front of the embassies of Pakistan and India every day to apply for a travel visa. Some sit in wheelchairs and others lay on gurneys as the visa officer calls out names. Some are shoved to the ground; others are beaten by security guards. The scene in front of these embassies is abhorrent. Millions of Afghans travel annually to Pakistan and India for medical

---

[10] "Cholecystectomy (Gallbladder Removal)," Department of Surgery, University of California-San Francisco, accessed 16 July 2021.

purposes. They need the most basic health services that are not available in Afghanistan.[11]

Amid the global COVID-19 pandemic, Facebook is filled with posts from those who have lost their loved ones to the virus. The official government tally significantly underrepresents what is happening on the ground.[12] According to personal stories, people with symptoms do not even go to the hospital to take the test, as they do not trust the health system. Those who have been tested do not get their results until weeks later. The previous government of Ashraf Ghani and now the Taliban have both failed to provide basic services such as oxygen to those in intensive care. Local news clips showed people purchasing oxygen tanks for thousands of Afghanis, while the previous government squandered a $100.4 million (USD) grant provided by the World Bank as part of the COVID-19 Emergency Response and Health Systems Preparedness Project.[13]

---

[11] Zabihullah Ghazi and Fahim Abed, "Demand for Pakistan Visas Sets Off Deadly Stampede in Afghanistan," *New York Times*, 27 October 2020. *Medical tourism*, or travel to another country for cheaper or better healthcare, is a growing industry for many nations. Poor healthcare facilities and the absence of certain technologies and expertise in Afghanistan have created an income stream for neighboring countries as Afghans cross their borders for medical treatment. See Gareth Price and Hameed Hakimi, *Reconnecting Afghanistan: Lessons from Cross-border Engagement* (London: Royal Institute of International Affairs, Chatham House, 2019).

[12] See "Afghanistan," Reuters COVID-19 Tracker, accessed 10 September 2021. The data on this site was provided by the Ministry of Public Health, Afghanistan.

[13] "World Bank Funds Transferred to the Government of the Islamic Republic of Afghanistan to Fight COVID-19 Pandemic," press release, World Bank, 20 April 2020.

The Nation-Building Strategy, 2009–16

In December 2009, President Obama put forth a comprehensive strategy for the war in Afghanistan. He traveled to the U.S. Military Academy at West Point, New York, to make his case to the nation and present his policy for this prolonged war as "the new way forward."[14]

First, Obama reiterated the fact that the United States never asked for this war, that it had been brought on by the terrorist attacks of 11 September 2001. While the hijackers who flew the commercial airliners into the World Trade Center and Pentagon were not Afghans, they had been trained in Afghanistan by a terrorist organization to attack the American homeland. Obama also shed light on the failures of the Afghan government, which was hampered by corruption, an underdeveloped economy, and insufficient security forces. The status quo was not sustainable, and something had to be done to change the course of the conflict in Afghanistan.[15]

Obama presented a timeline for U.S. involvement in the country. His military strategy was to increase troop levels on the ground to break the Taliban's momentum and increase Afghanistan's own military and police capacity to fight the Taliban and al-Qaeda thereafter.[16]

The president's economic development strategy focused on the following statement: "The days of providing a blank check are over." Instead, "America's effort in Afghanistan must be based on performance."[17] The days

---

[14] Barack H. Obama, "The New Way Forward—The President's Address" (speech, U.S. Military Academy at West Point, NY, 1 December 2009).

[15] Obama, "The New Way Forward."

[16] Obama, "The New Way Forward."

[17] Obama, "The New Way Forward."

of unaccountable spending and wasteful construction were over, according to this new policy. Nonetheless, Obama promised to increase development funding for Afghanistan through USAID.

Afghans on the streets of Kabul today would likely tell you that 2010 and 2011 were the best years for their businesses and livelihood. These two years mark a time when U.S. financial support to Afghanistan reached its peak. The trickle-down effect of such large sums of grants to the Afghan government was so significant that even ordinary fruit vendors on the side of the road benefited from increased business. Private and public construction projects boomed during this period, and many people working directly or indirectly for U.S. military or civilian contractors had large sums of disposable income.[18]

The question is whether this massive spending by the United States made any long-lasting impact on the Afghan economy. Did it help build a sustainable economy that would provide a decent living for ordinary Afghans for years to come without donor assistance?

The Second Afghan Presidential Election

President Obama's first major challenge in Afghanistan was not so much about his military posture against the Taliban and al-Qaeda but about the next Afghan presidential election.[19] For the United States and the world

---

[18] Jamieson Lesko, "Afghan Suburbia: Luxury Construction Boom Grips Kabul Despite Uncertain Future," NBC News, 28 September 2013.

[19] Ashley J. Tellis, *Reconciling with the Taliban?: Toward an Alternative Grand Strategy in Afghanistan* (Washington, DC: Carnegie Endowment for International Peace, 2009).

to maintain the democratic process that had been built in the country during the previous eight years, they had to make sure its second presidential election took place on time. President Hamid Karzai's first term was about to expire in July 2009, and under the Afghan constitution, elections had to be held no later than 60 days before the end of the presidential term.[20] However, voting was postponed by two months, reflecting the lack of strategic planning by the Afghan government and international donors. Karzai's term was extended until a new leader could be elected.[21]

The international community, including the United States, agreed to give $224 million (USD) for the 2009 Afghan presidential election.[22] According to the National Democratic Institute, approximately 4.6 million people turned out to vote on election day, which was considerably low compared to the 8 million who participated in 2004.[23] Observers reported low turnout of women, notably in certain polling stations in the southern and southeastern parts of the country where no women voted. Before the election, the Taliban had issued threats against anyone who participated in the election, including cutting off inked fingers, which fueled fear and resulted in low turnout among vot-

---

[20] Afghan Const. § 3, art. LXI says: "Elections for the new President shall be held within 30 to 60 days prior to the end of the presidential term."

[21] Jason Straziuso, "Afghan High Court Extends Karzai's Term 3 Months," *Toronto (Canada) Star*, 29 March 2009.

[22] *The 2009 Presidential and Provincial Council Elections* (Washington, DC: National Democratic Institute, 2010), 13.

[23] *The 2009 Presidential and Provincial Council Elections*, 37.

ers in general and among female voters in particular.[24]

Based on the total election budget and overall turn-out in the presidential election, the actual cost of each ballot was estimated at about $52 per vote, which would be the equivalent of one month's salary for a ordinary civil servant or the income of a street vendor who feeds a family of six or seven people.[25]

Ultimately, the election results were marred by widespread fraud and ballot box stuffing.[26] Following the election, the Independent Election Commission (IEC) of Afghanistan—the body in charge of the election—made various announcements of partial results. These results lacked transparency and fueled suspicion among international observers. Investigation by ob-servers revealed massive inconsistencies in the numbers provided by the IEC, and the partial results were be-lieved to be choreographed to tamper with the actual vote count.

Finally, after a month of deliberation, the prelimi-nary election results came out in favor of Karzai with 55 percent of the vote and Abdullah Abdullah with only 28 percent. After the Electoral Complaints Commission reviewed more than 3,000 complaints, the final presi-dential election results were announced in October, two months after the election.[27]

---

[24] Tyler Hicks, "Intimidation and Fraud Observed in Afghan Elec-tion," *New York Times*, 23 August 2009.

[25] *The 2009 Presidential and Provincial Council Elections.*

[26] Hicks, "Intimidation and Fraud Observed in Afghan Election."

[27] "Afghan Vote Results: Karzai at 54.6 Percent," NBC News, 16 September 2009. For more on the Electoral Complaints Commis-sion, see "Afghanistan: Electoral Complaints Commission," press release, United Nations Office for the Coordination of Humanitar-ian Affairs, 12 May 2009.

However, that was not the end of it. Abdullah did not concede and instead proclaimed himself the winner.[28] As a prominent Tajik leader, he used his base to stir up ethnic tensions, since Karzai was seen as more of a Pashtun leader.[29] Abdullah's actions could have possibly taken the country to the brink of yet another civil war. At this point, the Obama administration felt the need to intervene to avoid the unnecessary internal turmoil amid the war against the Taliban and al-Qaeda.

The Obama administration, through U.S. senator John F. Kerry (D-MA), mediated between the two contenders. After weeks of back and forth between Karzai and Abdullah, Kerry was able to convince both parties to participate in a runoff election. On 20 October, Karzai appeared at a press conference alongside Kerry, U.S. Ambassador to Afghanistan Karl W. Eikenberry, and United Nations (UN) Special Representative for Afghanistan Kai A. Eide to announce that he would participate in a runoff. However, a week later, Abdullah withdrew from the runoff, citing that adequate measures had not been taken to prevent the recurrence of fraud. The IEC canceled the runoff election and declared Karzai the winner of the 2009 presidential election.[30]

However, after Karzai was out of office, he said that unlike the administration of U.S. president George

---

[28] Jon Boone, "Afghanistan Election Challenger Abdullah Abdullah Pulls Out of Runoff," *Guardian*, 1 November 2009.

[29] For more on the differences between these two groups, see Abubakar Siddique, *Afghanistan's Ethnic Divides* (Oslo: Norwegian Peacebuilding Resource Centre, Norwegian Ministry of Foreign Affairs, 2012).

[30] John F. Kerry, "Senator Kerry on Afghanistan War," C-SPAN, 21 October 2009, 22:18 min.

W. Bush, the Obama administration was not on good terms with him. He believed that they wanted him removed from office during the 2009 presidential election. According to one of Karzai's associates, the U.S. special envoy for Afghanistan and Pakistan, Richard C. A. Holbrooke, was the main architect of the plot against the Afghan president.[31]

Clearly, democracy was still on very shaky ground in Afghanistan. Despite having spent millions of dollars on electoral processes and institutions, the country's election bodies still lacked the institutional capacity to carry out a nationwide election without causing suspicion on the outcome that could result in massive internal turmoil.

International Donor Conferences, 2009–16

During President Obama's time in office, three major international donor pledge conferences were held to solicit financial support for the development of Afghanistan. Since 2001, these conferences had become somewhat routine.[32] It had been more than a decade since the beginning of the war, and Afghanistan was still in need of development aid from the rest of the world. How did the international community and Afghan government fail to achieve sustainable development in Afghanistan? Why was the country still in need of foreign aid after 10 years, after 20 years?

On 12 June 2008, 68 countries and more than 15

---

[31] "Interview with Karim Khurram about His New Book," YouTube, 26 August 2019, 1:20:21 min.
[32] "A Historical Timeline of Afghanistan," PBS News Hour, 31 December 2014.

international organizations led by the United States attended the Paris Conference on Afghanistan. They pledged about $20 billion (USD) in aid for the country's development strategy for the next four years. The United States promised more than $10.2 billion in aid over two years, which was more than 50 percent of the overall pledge made by all other countries.[33] The Afghan government presented the *Afghanistan National Development Strategy* (ANDS) to the donors at this conference. The strategy outlined a list of commitments that would be achieved by 2013. The donors and the Afghan government agreed on a set of priorities to strengthen institutions and economic growth, particularly in agriculture and energy. They also endorsed the Afghanistan Compact, a set of ambitious goals agreed on at the London Conference a year prior that covered all sectors of security, governance, and development, including the cross-cutting goals of counternarcotics and regional cooperation.[34]

The *Afghanistan National Development Strategy* (2008–13) is a 200-page document that covers a broad array of issues, including policy direction, development strategy, aid effectiveness, coordination, and implementation framework. This document discusses every possible scenario and policy direction for poverty reduction, employment creation, economic growth, infrastructure, and private sector development. It includes a laundry list of issues that need to be addressed, but it reads as

---

[33] "Declaration of the International Conference in Support of Afghanistan," press release, United Nations, 12 June 2008, hereafter Paris declaration; and "Donors' Aid Pledges for Afghanistan," Reuters, 12 June 2008.

[34] Paris declaration.

yet another wish list from the Afghan government to donor countries for the sole purpose of soliciting further development aid or as a justification document for receiving the funds from mostly European countries and the United States.[35]

Following the Paris Conference, yet another conference was held in Tokyo in July 2012. Once again, major donor countries gathered and pledged to give Afghanistan another $16 billion (USD) in development aid through 2015, or approximately $4 billion annually. The United States reportedly made a commitment of $1–2 billion annually.[36] The difference this time was that there was no massive wish-list document like the ANDS, but rather a set of goals set forth by donors for the Afghan government to meet by the end of 2015 in exchange for the aid in the *Tokyo Mutual Accountability Framework* (TMAF).[37]

According to the Tokyo framework, the Afghan government and the international community had reaffirmed their partnership to focus on the economic growth and development of Afghanistan through a process of mutual accountability in achieving jointly decided goals. The aid was conditional based on the delivery of each commitment outlined in the framework. One of the main pillars of the TMAF was to help direct the Afghan government and the economy toward self-reliance. As part of that effort, the Afghan government

---

[35] *Afghanistan National Development Strategy: First Annual Report (2008/09)* (Washington, DC: International Monetary Fund, 2009).
[36] Katerina Oskarsson, *Second International Tokyo Conference on Afghanistan* (Brussels, Belgium: Civil-Military Fusion Centre, North Atlantic Treaty Organization, 2012).
[37] "Tokyo Mutual Accountability Framework," USAID, 8 July 2012.

was given more ownership of projects. In exchange, donors requested that the Afghan government put together a list of National Priority Programs (NPP). The idea was to ensure optimal execution and effectiveness of international assistance aligned with national priorities that the government deemed necessary. The Tokyo framework outlined 16 benchmarks that needed to be achieved for the Afghan government to receive the full pledged amount of $16 billion.[38]

Four years later, yet another international pledging conference was scheduled to take place on 5 October 2016 in Brussels. The European Union agreed to cohost the conference with the government of Afghanistan to bring in the international community to reaffirm their commitment to the development of Afghanistan. More than 75 countries and 26 international organizations and agencies participated in the conference and pledged approximately $15 billion (USD) for the next four years.[39]

The author helped facilitate technical arrangements for the Brussels Conference. As part of the policy team at the Ministry of Finance in Afghanistan, he and his associates worked closely with the international donor countries, particularly with the European Union, in Kabul a year in advance to plan for the conference. Unlike previous events, the international community now had more confidence in the capacity of Afghans to lead the groundwork for the conference. Afghans who had stud-

---

[38] "Tokyo Mutual Accountability Framework."

[39] "Brussels Conference on Afghanistan: October 4–5, 2016," Bureau of South and Central Asian Affairs, Department of State, 12 December 2016.

ied in the United States, Europe, or Australia were back in Afghanistan and were working for the government. Afghan president Ashraf Ghani's first-term administration made considerable efforts to appeal to people to come work in Afghanistan. These Western-educated Afghans took on responsibilities that were once fulfilled by international expats who received significant compensation and other benefits, representing one of the ways that large sums of aid money given to the Afghan people vanished and ended up back in Europe and America. An ordinary technical staff member who had received an annual salary of $80,000–$85,000 in the United States was making three to four times that amount in Afghanistan. However, the newly Western-educated Afghans held those jobs at a fraction of the cost to either the Afghan government or American taxpayers.[40]

Hundreds of thousands of young Afghans received scholarships to study abroad in the last 20 years, which is regarded as one of Afghanistan's best success stories.[41] The author came to the United States as a high school exchange student through a program sponsored by the U.S. Department of State. He was a part of the first group of 40 Afghan students to arrive in the United States following the 11 September 2001 terrorist attacks. The American government and families who had

---

[40] *Fighting Corruption in Afghanistan: A Roadmap for Strategy and Action* (n.p.: Asian Development Bank, UK Department for International Development, United Nations Development Programme, United Nations Office on Drugs and Crime, and the World Bank, 2007).

[41] "Kennedy-Lugar Youth Exchange & Study Program," World Learning, accessed 19 July 2021.

agreed to host the students for the school year greeted them with open arms. The author's personal experience shows that a small initial investment in Afghanistan's education sector has the potential for a significant snowball effect. Those who participated in the exchange program are now highly qualified individuals who have either returned to Afghanistan to work or are contributing to their country of birth from afar.

Afghanistan: An Amazingly Young Country

Despite its difficulties, Afghanistan is a young and growing country. According to Index Mundi, the latest demographic data from Afghanistan shows that 63.5 percent of the population is younger than 24 years. There are 7.6 million Afghan children between the ages of 10 and 19 who are poised to enter higher education in the next few years.[42] Today, the average age of the Afghan population is 18.6 years.[43] This offers an amazing opportunity for Afghanistan because it comes at a time when the rest of the world is aging.

According to some estimates, the average age of the population in India is 29 years; in Pakistan, 25 years; in China, 40 years; in Europe, 46 years; in the United States, 40; and in Afghanistan, 20.[44] These young Afghans are poised to transform their country and the world's faith. Afghanistan will have approximately 12

---

[42] "Afghanistan Demographics Profile," Index Mundi, accessed 31 May 2021.

[43] Richard Giasy, "The Afghan People: Observing Nearly 40 Years of Violent Conflict," *Write Peace* (blog), SIPRI, 5 October 2017.

[44] "Median Age of the World Population from 1990 to 2015 and a Forecast until 2100, by Fertility Variant," Statista, accessed 19 July 2021.

million people in the 20–24 age group entering the labor force, whereas most other developed countries will have a significant labor force deficit.[45] While the opportunity is there for young Afghans to take, it remains to be seen as to whether they are prepared to seize the opportunity.

If Afghanistan can equip, educate, and train its younger generation, it will not only transform its own economy and society but also possibly impact the world. If Afghanistan fails to capitalize on this opportunity, the demographic dividend discussed here will transform into a demographic disaster. Recent history has made clear what happens when unemployed, dissatisfied, and uneducated young people fall victim to the Islamic State and the Taliban's propaganda machines. In this interconnected world, education is more than just a social or economic issue for Afghans—it is also a national security issue on a global scale.

Initially, following the fall of the Taliban regime, the Afghan government needed to expand the higher education system. According to the World Bank, three decades of war and devastation had left Afghans with a 17-percent literacy rate.[46] In early 2001, there were only 7,800 students enrolled in the higher education system at no more than seven universities in the country.[47] As a result, growth was critical. By 2015, Afghanistan's literacy rate had increased to 58 percent, student enrollment had increased to 174,424, and the number of universities had increased to 76. Thus, in the 20 years since the

[45] "Afghanistan: Overview," World Bank, accessed 31 May 2021.
[46] "Afghanistan: Overview."
[47] "Education System Profiles: Education in Afghanistan," World Education News & Reviews, 6 September 2016.

Taliban, a tremendous amount of expansion took place. However, one out of every three school-age children was still absent from the classroom.[48] The system's expansion did not go far enough, and it failed to educate everyone.

In the aftermath of the Taliban, the Afghan government strove for equity, including those previously excluded from education, and attempted to connect with those who had previously been unreachable. During the Taliban's reign in the 1990s, female literacy had been close to zero.[49] There were no female students enrolled in school. The government and international donor agencies made significant efforts to improve this statistic; however, in some areas of Afghanistan, the enrollment rate for females is still zero. It is now incumbent on the Taliban to reach out to those rural areas and provide educational opportunities for women and disadvantaged students, while also allowing male and female students in major cities to return to school.

How has Afghanistan fared in terms of getting the expansion and equity sides of the formula right? The education system still requires improvement. Several post-Taliban universities, including the American University of Afghanistan and Kardan University, provide high-quality education in Kabul. However, the average Afghan higher education institution is simply not of the expected quality. Students who have graduated from the majority of these institutions are still unemployed.[50] They

---

[48] "Education System Profiles: Education in Afghanistan."

[49] Emma Graham-Harrison and Akhtar Mohammad Makoii, " 'The Taliban Took Years of My Life': The Afghan Women Living in the Shadow of War," *Guardian*, 9 February 2019.

[50] *"I Won't Be a Doctor, and One Day You'll Be Sick": Girls' Access to Education in Afghanistan* (New York: Human Rights Watch, 2017).

do not have the necessary skills for the jobs available. Some businesses and ministries provide capacity-building training to compensate for basic skill deficiencies required for the job. Improving the quality of secondary and tertiary education is a critical government task.

Overall, Afghanistan must prepare its young people for the challenges of the twenty-first century. In the age of Google, where information can be found with the click of a mouse, they require not only new graduates with a quality education but also a workforce that is well-rounded and trained to support the ever-changing labor market. The workforce must be able to react to unfamiliar facts and details and be capable of synthesizing information that has not been studied. There is no doubt that the challenges are massive.

In preparation for the Brussels Conference, just as with the Paris Conference of 2008 where the Afghan government presented donors with the *Afghanistan National Development Strategy*, President Ghani and his new administration were committed to displaying a similar declaration to donors. The technical team was assigned to work on a comprehensive strategy paper called the *Afghanistan National Peace and Development Framework (ANPDF) 2017 to 2021*. The theme of the document was self-reliance through sustainable economic development that will help Afghanistan bring an end to poverty.[51] The author was tasked with creating a five-year infrastructure plan for Afghanistan as part of a

---

[51] "Communique on the Brussels Conference on Afghanistan," press release, Department of State, 5 October 2016; and *Afghanistan National Peace and Development Framework (ANPDF) 2017 to 2021* (Kabul: Ministry of Finance, Islamic Republic of Afghanistan, 2016).

major push by the government to draw more aid to the education sector and beyond.

Infrastructure was considered a vital sector by Ghani and his team. During the 2014 Afghan presidential campaign, Ghani published a 309-page election manifesto in which he envisioned infrastructure development through the prism of regional connectivity.[52] The author's job was to develop a five-year roadmap for achieving that vision.

Putting together this massive document was no simple matter. The first task was to bring together all the relevant ministries of the government and discuss what they deemed most important for infrastructure development. This informal conference was meant to include members from the Ministry of Urban Development and Housing, the Ministry of Mines and Petroleum, the Ministry of Transport and Civil Aviation, the Ministry of Commerce and Industry, the Independent Directorate of Local Governance, and several others. Ultimately, however, none of these groups were willing to participate, either because they did not have a plan for relevant infrastructure development in their sectors or because they did not want to share it. They did, however, submit multipage documents laying out what they thought infrastructure development meant for them. None of the information helped craft the infrastructure plan, however.[53] An infrastructure plan had never been developed for the country in the past.

---

[52] Ahmadzai Ghani, *Manifesto of Change and Continuity Team* (Kabul: Islamic Republic of Afghanistan, 2014).

[53] *National Infrastructure Plan, 2017–2021* (Kabul: Ministry of Finance, Islamic Republic of Afghanistan, 2016).

The next step was to seek assistance from the Asian Development Bank (ADB), which had made significant investments in Afghanistan's infrastructure development during the previous decade. Thanks in large part to the ADB for providing the author with the technical support for producing the infrastructure plan, the working group was able to put together a compressive investment pipeline for 2017–21 that focused on the efficient planning, delivery, and operation of infrastructure at the national and local levels.[54]

Finding a mechanism to reach international maritime markets is critical for Afghanistan, a landlocked country (figure 24). Pakistan and Iran have both used their trade lines as political leverage over the Afghan government in the post-Taliban era and they continue to do so now. In retribution for the killing of 24 Pakistani soldiers by a U.S. unmanned drone in November 2011, Pakistan's government decided to restrict the supply lines to Afghanistan. Thousands of containers loaded with commercial items heading for Afghanistan were stranded at the Port of Karachi. Businesses suffered significant losses as perishable items rotted and nonperishables were grounded for weeks.[55]

Afghanistan recorded a 77-percent trade imbalance last year with a $3.2 billion (USD) trade deficit as a result of these difficulties.[56] To address the lack of sea

---

[54] *Afghanistan: Improving the Development Effectiveness of the Afghanistan Infrastructure Trust Fund* (Manila, Philippines: Asian Development Bank, 2020).

[55] "Pakistan Outrage after 'Nato Attack Kills Soldiers'," BBC News, 26 November 2011.

[56] "Afghanistan Products Exports, Imports, Tariffs by Country and Region, 2018," WITS Data, World Bank, accessed 19 July 2021.

Figure 24. Supply routes through Pakistan

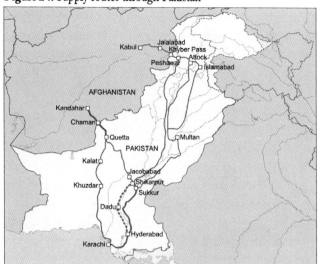

Source: map courtesy of NordNordWest, adapted by MCUP.

access, the Afghan government developed a five-year infrastructure development blueprint for the first time, highlighting structural challenges for the country and the path forward for transforming Afghanistan from a landlocked to land-connected country, as Ghani had proposed in his election manifesto.[57]

Afghanistan's infrastructure continues to be a major barrier to the country's global success. Despite large infrastructure investments and improvements since 2002, poor transportation connectivity, regional market integration hurdles, insufficient legislative and regulatory changes, institutional capacity, and human skill limits

---

[57] Ghani, *Manifesto of Change and Continuity Team.*

restrict economic growth. Regional market integration difficulties, insufficient policy and regulatory reforms, institutional capacity and human skill limits, persistent security issues, and limited operations and maintenance funds for existing infrastructure were all significant constraints.

The *National Infrastructure Plan, 2017–2021* (NIP) outlined the government's ideas for improving infrastructure investment efficiency. The NIP included an infrastructure investment pipeline to aid in the development of a transportation network system. The pipeline was intended to enhance the country's economic development by increasing access to domestic, regional, and worldwide markets. This included rail and road investments, such as the Kabul Ring Road, border road links, the Salang Tunnel in the Hindu Kush mountain range, and road operations and maintenance projects. It also extended to urban transportation, civil aviation, trade facilitation, dry ports, and transport logistics. The plan detailed a road map for regional connectivity, including efficient infrastructure delivery that created jobs and linked goods to markets in Afghanistan and the region.[58]

Regional connectedness would be achieved by enhanced transportation networks, freight and logistics supply chains, energy supplies, and high-speed telecommunications. Afghanistan must become a regional hub that connects Central Asia and South Asia, as well as China and Europe, in an east-westerly route to reap the benefits of its geographic dividend.[59] The *National Infrastructure Plan* streamlines the following invest-

---

[58] *National Infrastructure Plan, 2017–2021.*
[59] *National Infrastructure Plan, 2017–2021.*

ments to promote regional possibilities with significant domestic returns and benefits.

Moving Energy

Afghanistan was meant to be a utility corridor connecting Central Asia's energy-rich countries with South Asia's energy-poor countries. Three projects were in the works:

- The Turkmenistan-Afghanistan-Pakistan (TAP) power transmission line, which would deliver 2,000 megawatts (mw) of electricity from Turkmenistan to Pakistan via western Afghanistan, with the capacity to expand to 4,000 mw in the future.
- The Turkmenistan-Afghanistan-Pakistan-India (TAPI) gas pipeline, which would carry natural gas from Turkmenistan to Pakistan and India via Afghanistan.
- The Central Asia-South Asia (CASA)-1000 transmission lines, which would transport more than 1,000 mw of electricity from Kyrgyzstan and Tajikistan to Pakistan via Afghanistan.[60]

These three programs built on previous work and were in the process of increasing regional bulk energy transfers. The projects would require significant funding, with the TAP costing an estimated $500 million (USD) and the TAPI costing an estimated $12.5 billion, with

---

[60] *National Infrastructure Plan, 2017–2021*, 7.

Figure 25. TAP and CASA-1000 projects map

Source: USAID and United Nations Economic Commission for Europe.

$7 billion coming from private sources. The estimated cost of CASA-1000 was $1.17 billion (figure 25).[61]

In the coming decade, Pakistan is estimated to require more than 15,000 mw of extra electricity.[62] The aforementioned projects are well-positioned to supply

[61] *National Infrastructure Plan, 2017–2021*, 42.
[62] Saleem Shaikh and Sughra Tunio, "Pakistan Ramps up Coal Power with Chinese-backed Plants," Reuters, 2 May 2017.

an economically feasible energy source from Central Asian countries with abundant energy resources to Pakistan via Afghanistan. This is a critical part of how regional connection may benefit not only Afghanistan but the entire region.

The primary goal was getting products and merchandise across Afghanistan to the rest of the region. The importance of regional trade connectivity and the national goal of completing the Ring Road were reflected in the *National Infrastructure Plan*'s transportation sector priorities. Three of the six Central Asia Regional Economic Cooperation Program (CAREC) corridors had a key link running parallel to motorways in Afghanistan. Afghanistan would also lie along the corridor connecting Tajikistan via Sher Khan Bandar (Kunduz Province) to Islam Qala (Herat Province), which connects to Iran, as part of China's "One Belt One Road" initiative.[63] Later in 2017, the Turkmen railroad arrived at Aqina, Afghanistan. This paved the way for the Lapis Lazuli Corridor, which provided an alternative route for products from China, as well as imports and exports from Afghanistan, to reach Europe via Turkmenistan and the Caspian Sea. By connecting these regional transit links, Afghanistan's proposed railroad beltway would open up new economic potential.[64]

---

[63] For more on China's infrastructure initiative, see Andrew Scobell et al., *At the Dawn of Belt and Road: China in the Developing World* (Santa Monica, CA: Rand, 2018), https://doi.org/10.7249/RR2273.

[64] Mariam Safi and Bismellah Alizada, *Integrating Afghanistan into the Belt and Road Initiative: Review, Analysis and Prospects* (Bonn, Germany: Friedrich Ebert Stiftung, 2018).

The national railway plan saw prospects for railway spurs to Pakistan via Torkham (Nangarhar Province) and Spin Boldak (Kandahar Province) ports, which would help move commodities from Pakistan to Central Asian countries. Similarly, with the development of the Charbahar (Iran) and Gwadar (Pakistan) ports, Afghanistan may become the most cost-effective path for Central Asian countries to access international markets and connect with the Arabian Peninsula and beyond for both imports and exports.

Moving Data

Because Asia and Europe account for roughly one-half of all internet traffic, the future is filled with data transfer opportunities. The current data transfer channel uses a maritime fiber that spans the Mediterranean, passes through the Suez Canal and the Red Sea, and wraps around Asian markets at a rate of about 15 terabytes per second.[65] This path has a number of issues. First, maritime cables are more susceptible to constant maintenance, damage, and entities being able to harness the cable. Second, due to the long pathway, data transfer takes approximately 130 milliseconds, which is extremely slow.[66]

By increasing internet connectivity and modernizing relevant policies and regulatory frameworks, the digital CASA program and fiber optic networks were viewed as lifelines for the telecommunications sector. Due to the high costs of internet packages, internet penetration

---

[65] Associated Press, "Finger-thin Undersea Cables Tie World Together," NBC News, 31 January 2008.
[66] *Enhancing Connectivity and Freight in Central Asia: Case-Specific Policy Analysis*, International Transport Forum Policy Papers No. 71 (Paris, France: OECD Publishing, 2019).

remains low across CASA countries, despite significant levels of mobile cellular usage.[67] Following the Afghan government's approval of an open-access policy to end the existing monopoly in the telecommunications sector, companies were able to actively invest and, where necessary, form public-private partnerships. As a result, costs would be reduced while user services and access would be expanded.[68]

These connectivity projects have the potential to generate significant revenue for the transit system. In the long term, the proposed data movement (TASEM and digital CASA) could generate hundreds of millions of dollars.[69] TAP is expected to generate $200 million or more, while CASA-1000 transit fees are expected to generate $40 million.[70]

The *National Infrastructure Plan, 2017–2021*, proposed a pipeline of ongoing and new projects. The strategy was to increase the efficiency of infrastructure investment while also including new projects with the potential for public-private partnership participation. The project selection criteria included economic and social benefits (direct and indirect), income growth, employment and poverty reduction, sustainability, security risk environment, and regional connectivity prospects. The total cost of the projects was estimated to be around $6 billion (USD), with infrastructure development projects requiring $1 billion per year.[71] This was the amount

---

[67] *Enhancing Connectivity and Freight in Central Asia.*

[68] *National Infrastructure Plan, 2017–2021.*

[69] TASEM refers to technology assisted science, engineering, and mathematics.

[70] *National Infrastructure Plan, 2017–2021*, 7.

[71] *National Infrastructure Plan, 2017–2021*, 15.

the Afghan government planned to ask donors for at the Brussels conference.

One of the two major side events at the conference—the regional economic cooperation event—was designated for presenting the *National Infrastructure Plan*. High-level representatives from more than 25 countries and 15 multilateral organizations attended the gathering. President Ghani was invited as a keynote speaker. The opening remarks were given by the European commissioner for international cooperation and development, Neven Mimica, and the vice president of the ADB, Wencai Zhang. Following Ghani's keynote address, in which he spoke about the importance of Afghanistan's geographical location in helping facilitate the economic integration of the region, the president's chief advisor, Mohammad Humayon Qayoumi, presented the *National Infrastructure Plan*.[72] The overall response to the presentation of the infrastructure roadmap was very positive, and donor countries agreed to pay the requested amount for infrastructure development: $1 billion per year for five years.

However, it has been five years since the Brussels conference took place, and none of the aforementioned projects have come to fruition. One of the main reasons for this lack of progress is the scarcity of human capital in government ministries tasked to develop and initiate the projects. According to the Ministry of Finance's General Directorate of Budget, the Afghan government ministries were able to spend only 67 percent of their

---

[72] "Brussels Conference on Afghanistan: Realizing Afghanistan's Economic Potential and Reinforcing the Role of Women," press release, European Commission, 4 October 2016.

total development budget in 2017, 73 percent in 2018, and 85 percent in 2019.[73] They were not able to spend the $1.6 billion (USD) in the last three years that was allotted to them in the national budget. Some of this money had come directly from Afghan government revenue, but more than 80 percent of the overall development budget for these line ministries had been provided by donors as nondiscretionary funds (figure 26).

Lack of expertise within these ministries is one critical issue. Corruption is yet another problem that hinders progress in Afghanistan. According to the most recent Integrity Watch Afghanistan survey, more than 4.6 million Afghans paid some sort of bribe in 2018 (figure 27). That is an increase of about 35 percent in the last two years.[74] Moreover, the total amount of bribes paid in 2018 amounted to more than $1.65 billion (USD), which is about 9 percent of the total GDP of Afghanistan (figure 28).[75] The study also highlights that the decline in the total value of bribes by about 43 percent since 2016 is due to two main reasons:

> *with a significant increase in the proportion of Afghans living below the national poverty line from 38 percent in 2011/12 to 55 percent in 2016/17—which may mean that citizens' ability to pay bribes has weakened . . . and possibly the success-*

---

[73] *The Budget and Expenditures for the Development of Economic Analysis* (Kabul: Ministry of Finance, Islamic Republic of Afghanistan, 2020).

[74] *National Corruption Survey, 2018: Afghans' Perceptions and Experiences of Corruption* (Kabul: Integrity Watch Afghanistan, 2018), 39.

[75] Zabihullah Jahanmal, "Afghans Paid $1.6 Billion in Bribes in 2018: Report," TOLO News, 29 June 2020.

Figure 26. Development budget expenditures, 2017–19, percentage

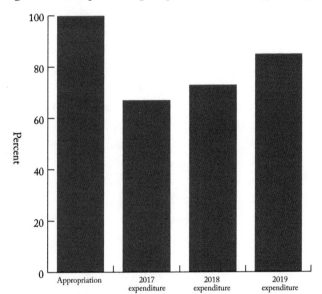

Source: *The Budget and Expenditures for the Development of Economic Analysis* (Kabul: Ministry of Finance, Islamic Republic of Afghanistan, 2020).

ful implementation of government anti-corruption reform strategies.[76]

One of SIGAR's quarterly reports published in July 2018 indicated that the Anti-Corruption Justice Center (ACJC), which was established by President Ghani in May 2016 as a new judicial body targeting corruption, has shown little ability to function as intended. More than 100 ACJC warrants are outstanding, while near-

[76] *National Corruption Survey, 2018,* 38.

Figure 27. Number of people who paid bribes, 2012–18, millions

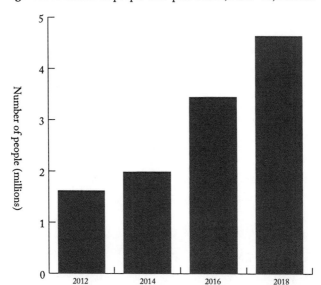

Source: *April–June 2019 Quarterly Report to the People of Afghanistan* (Kabul: Independent Joint Anti-Corruption Monitoring and Evaluation Committee, 2019).

ly 40 percent of the prosecutors assigned to the ACJC have failed polygraphs, seriously undermining the agency's legitimacy.[77] In addition, the 2018 SIGAR report to Congress noted that the ACJC is attempting to placate donors by pursuing several low-level corruption cases rather than the high-level corruption cases that are its mandate.[78]

---

[77] *Quarterly Report to the United States Congress, July 30, 2018* (Arlington, VA: Special Inspector General for Afghanistan Reconstruction, 2018), 20.

[78] *Quarterly Report to the United States Congress, July 30, 2018*, 125.

Figure 28. Total amount of bribes paid, 2012–18, USD billions

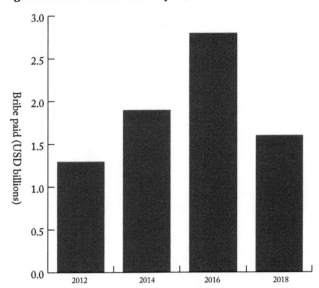

Source: *April–June 2019 Quarterly Report to the People of Afghanistan* (Kabul: Independent Joint Anti-Corruption Monitoring and Evaluation Committee, 2019).

While the international community generously opened their wallets at the Brussels conference, the Afghan government failed to deliver on what it had promised to the people of Afghanistan and international aid donors. In addition to the infrastructure projects proposed, the Afghan government came to an agreement with the donors at the conference on a set of deliverables called the *Self-Reliance through Mutual Accountability Framework (SMAF)*. Under SMAF, there was a total of 24 indicators for the Afghan government to accomplish by a set timeframe of two or four years. Anticorruption strategy, fair and transparent elections, and reduction of poverty were the top three international community requests in addition to a women's economic empowerment plan and the establishment of a special court division on violence against women. Ultimately, a significant number of the commitments made in the Brussels conference in 2016 have yet to be achieved.[79]

---

[79] *Self-Reliance through Mutual Accountability Framework (SMAF)* (Kabul: Islamic Republic of Afghanistan, 2015).

CHAPTER FIVE

The Cost of War

According to the United States Agency for International Development (USAID), the United States spent more than $76 billion between 2008 and 2016, most of which occurred during the administration of U.S. president Barack H. Obama.[1] The money was primarily appropriated for development purposes and not for military operations. Afghanistan remained the top recipient of USAID aid throughout this period, receiving on average approximately $9.5 billion per year.[2] As underscored in figure 29, the amount of aid increased each year and plateaued at $13 billion in 2012–13. That represents a 44-percent increase from the $9 billion in aid delivered in 2009. The Obama administration's counterinsurgency policy was coupled with humanitarian assistance in the forms of grants and development aid through USAID to win the hearts and minds of the locals. As a result of this massive surge in troops and additional financial support to the government of Afghanistan, U.S. development assistance during Obama's presidency increased by 250 percent compared to that of his predecessor, George W. Bush.[3]

In 2012, the Obama administration's interest in fighting the Taliban and al-Qaeda began to wane. The U.S. presidential election that year was one of the key

---

[1] "Foreign Aid Explorer," USAID, 2021.
[2] "Foreign Aid Explorer."
[3] "Foreign Aid Explorer."

Figure 29. Obama-era aid to Afghanistan, 2009–16, USD millions

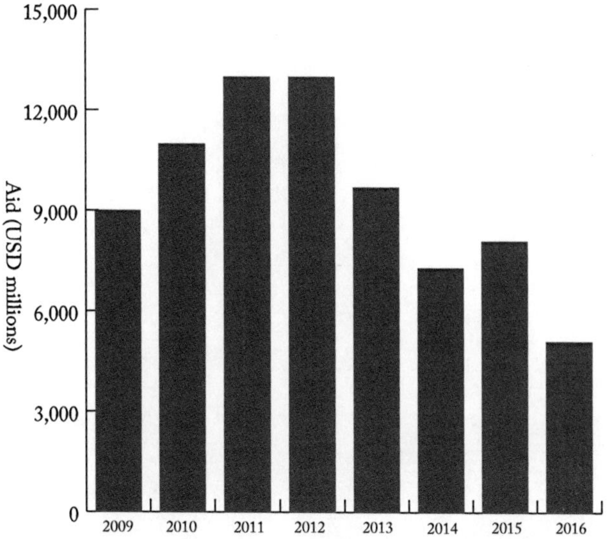

Source: "Foreign Aid Explorer," USAID, 2021.

reasons for the decline in interest in the Afghanistan conflict. According to a *Washington Post*-ABC News poll conducted in early 2011, nearly three-quarters of Americans believed Obama should withdraw a "substantial number" of combat troops from Afghanistan.[4] In May 2012, he flew to Bagram Air Base in Afghanistan to sign a strategic partnership agreement with Afghan president Hamid Karzai that established the terms of their relationship following the withdrawal

---

[4] Scott Wilson and Jon Cohen, "Poll: Nearly Two-thirds of Americans Say Afghan War Isn't Worth Fighting," *Washington Post*, 15 March 2011.

of American troops in 2014.[5] It was an opportunity for President Obama to make an election-year case that he was winding down a costly and increasingly unpopular war at home during a heated political campaign season.

Moreover, the war in Afghanistan was not going as expected. The Obama administration's relationship with the Karzai government, which had not been good from the start, had been further eroded by mistrust. Karzai's chief of staff said in an interview that the Obama administration did not want Karzai to win a second term in 2009.[6] Subsequently, the Karzai team viewed American actions in Afghanistan with suspicion and never really bonded with their U.S. counterparts as they had with the Bush administration. In late 2012, when the author was working at the Afghanistan embassy in Washington, DC, the diplomatic relationship of the embassy with the U.S. Department of State suffered significantly. U.S. officials did not show the willingness to meet with Afghan embassy officials as often as before, which resulted in a lack of interest in the Afghanistan War and development efforts.[7]

Figure 29 shows an incremental annual decrease in USAID funds to Afghanistan beginning in 2013, cutting back more than 25 percent in one year from $13 billion to $9.7 billion (USD). By the end of Obama's second term in office in 2016, the total U.S. development aid to Afghanistan decreased to about $5.1 bil-

---

[5] Mark Landler, "Obama Signs Pact in Kabul, Turning Page in Afghan War," *New York Times*, 2 May 2012.
[6] Michele Kelemen, "Relationship between Karzai, U.S. Deteriorates," NPR, 8 April 2010.
[7] Kelemen, "Relationship between Karzai, U.S. Deteriorates."

Figure 30. U.S. aid funding allocations, 2008–16, by sector

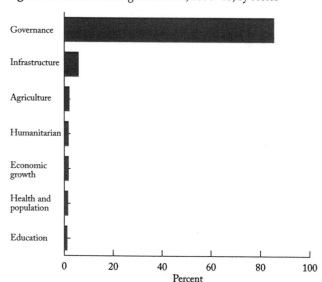

Source: "Foreign Aid Explorer," USAID, 2021.

lion, a 40-percent drop from when he came into office in 2009.[8]

U.S. Aid Allocation, 2008–16

According to the USAID database, 85 percent of the total \$76 billion given by the United States to Afghanistan between 2008 and 2016 had been allocated to governance-related projects, while only 1.27 percent of the funding was designated for education (figure 30). Further breakdown of governance-related programs in-

[8] "Foreign Aid Explorer."

Figure 31. Governance projects, 2008–16

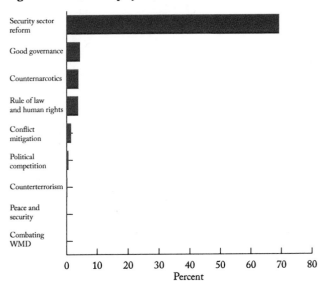

Source: "Foreign Aid Explorer," USAID, 2021.

dicates that the security sector reform program, which is designed primarily to support the Afghan National Police (ANP) and Afghan National Army (ANA), absorbed $53 billion, or 69 percent, of the total aid amount (figure 31).[9]

Unfortunately, the sectors for infrastructure, private sector development, education, and health did not receive the kind of funding they needed to flourish. While the majority of the USAID funding was allocated for security sector reform, a lack of oversight and accountability of the program allowed for massive corruption

---

[9] "Foreign Aid Explorer."

and fraud. As a result, the ANP and ANA were not up to the task to defend and secure Afghanistan when the Taliban retook control of the country in August 2021.

In 2019, Afghan president Ashraf Ghani said at the World Economic Forum in Davos, Switzerland, that "over 45,000 Afghan security personnel have paid the ultimate sacrifice" since he had become president.[10] This is a staggering casualty figure, equating to nearly 50 deaths a day. The number of ANP and ANA servicemembers killed had continued to increase after the withdrawal of international combat troops in 2014. Rising death tolls could also have been due to increasing insurgent attacks. However, if the troops were well equipped and trained, the number of casualties could have been much lower.

A recent Special Inspector General for Afghanistan Reconstruction (SIGAR) report summarizes clearly how little U.S. efforts to develop the Afghan national security forces have achieved in the last two decades:

> *the United States failed to implement—in coordination with Afghan leadership and NATO partners—a stable and comprehensive ANDSF [Afghan National Defense and Security Forces] force design that would guide the long-term structure of the U.S. advisory effort. Without a long-term plan that detailed desired operational capabilities, equipping decisions were often ad hoc and inconsistent from year to year. Commanders serving one-year rotations prioritized the tactical fight*

---

[10] "Afghanistan's Ghani Says 45,000 Security Personnel Killed since 2014," BBC News, 25 January 2019.

*and equipped the ANDSF with little re-
gard for past equipping decisions or future
expenses.*[11]

In addition to a lack of sustainable development in
the security sector, the report also highlights the fact
that, while the U.S. government provided close to $5 bil-
lion a year in security sector assistance to Afghanistan,
without a reduction in violence through a political settlement or expansion of the Afghan government's ability to increase revenue through taxes, Afghan security
forces' sustainability would be fully reliant on donors.[12]
In a CBS *60 Minutes* interview, Ghani said, "We will
not be able to support our army for six months without
the U.S. support, and U.S. capabilities."[13] Hence, after
20 years and more than $200 billion spent on build-
ing Afghan security forces capacities and capabilities,
the situation was as dire when the Taliban fighters en-
croached on Kabul in August 2021 as it was in 2001, if
not more so.

Had the United States invested more in the economic growth and education sectors, the situation
might have been dramatically different. A proverb says
that if you give a poor man a fish, you feed him for a day,
but if you teach him to fish, you find him an occupation

---

[11] *Divided Responsibility: Lessons from U.S. Security Sector Assistance
Efforts in Afghanistan* (Arlington, VA: SIGAR, 2019), 144.
[12] *Divided Responsibility*, 145.
[13] Lara Logan, "Kabul under Siege while America's Longest War
Rages On," *60 Minutes*, CBS News, 14 January 2018.

that will feed him for a lifetime.[14] This concept runs parallel to the issues of development aid to Afghanistan.

Unofficial unemployment numbers in Afghanistan was roughly about 35–40 percent prior to the U.S.-backed government collapse. Young students graduate with advanced degrees from public and private universities in hopes of obtaining a job and making a decent living.[15] However, most went from one government ministry building to another in search of a higher-level official who would hire them. When the author was in Kabul, he would receive calls from relatives who wanted him to find them a job at the Ministry of Finance. It was not until sometime later that the author realized this is the only way for many people to find employment—one had to know someone in the government to get a job. Occupations in the private sector were very limited or nonexistent, so people primarily relied on scarce government work. Afghanistan has never been known for production. It has always been heavily reliant on goods imported from neighboring countries. While new jobs are being created in Iran and Pakistan as a

---

[14] There is some debate about the origin of this saying. Though many have long believed that it is a Chinese proverb, there is no evidence tying it to China. It likely originated in England in the 1880s by Anne Isabella Ritchie, the daughter of William Makepeace Thackeray, who wrote in her novel *Mrs. Dymond*, "He certainly doesn't practise [*sic*] his precepts, but I suppose the patron meant that if you give a man a fish he is hungry again in an hour; if you teach him to catch a fish you do him a good turn." Miss Thackery, *Mrs. Dymond*, vol. 1 (Leipzig: Bernhard Tauchnitz, 1886).

[15] "Unemployment Rate Spikes in Afghanistan," TOLO News, 2 October 2015.

result of increased exports to Afghanistan, the Afghan economy remains stagnant, and young people in the country are unemployed.[16]

Afghanistan has developed an economic relationship that is reliant on Pakistan and Iran as a result of its underdeveloped private sector. Since 2001, Pakistan has become the largest exporter to Afghanistan, with annual exports of approximately $1.7 billion (USD).[17] Conversely, Pakistan is a major export market for Afghanistan's raw materials, with approximately $71 million exported to Pakistan each year, accounting for 21.8 percent of all Afghan exports.[18] With more than $1 billion in exports to Afghanistan in 2018, Iran has surpassed the United States as the second-largest exporter. However, the vast bulk of Afghanistan's exports to Pakistan and Iran are raw materials that are processed and used in consumer goods before being resold to Afghans at a higher price.[19]

The Afghan economy has remained underdeveloped partially as a result of this disproportionate transaction with its neighbors. Due to high import prices and high unemployment, young Afghan men have been forced to migrate to Iran and Pakistan in search of work. Usually, they are exploited, abused, tortured, and humiliated. They typically enter these countries illegally and without a work visa. The United Nations

---

[16] "Afghanistan: Overview," World Bank, accessed 20 July 2021; and "Afghanistan (AFG): Exports, Imports, and Trade Partners," OEC, 2019.

[17] "Pakistan and Afghanistan," Institute for the Study of War, accessed 20 July 2021.

[18] "Pakistan and Afghanistan."

[19] "Pakistan and Afghanistan."

High Commissioner for Refugees (UNHCR) inter-
viewed 784 Afghans deported from Iran and Pakistan,
the vast majority of whom were single men.[20] According
to one of the survey's main findings, "the high rate of
unemployment, low wages, and widespread poverty in
Afghanistan are the major push factors for single men
to migrate to Iran and Pakistan." The current migration
flow between Afghanistan, Pakistan, and Iran is primarily a labor migration issue rather than a refugee issue.[21]

The number of undocumented Afghans in Iran
and Pakistan is unknown. However, during the last
two years, Iranian authorities have deported more than
700,000 Afghans who they claim violated immigration
laws and were working there illegally.[22] An estimated $500 million (USD) in remittances is sent back to
Afghanistan each year from Iran alone, accounting for
roughly 6 percent of Afghanistan's national GDP.[23]

Those young men who cannot afford to leave Afghanistan to avoid the unemployment problem remain
in the country. This segment of the population is extremely vulnerable and easily exploited by insurgents.
According to a recent report by the European Asylum
Support Office, "joblessness, poverty and the government's inattention has left youth with few other op-

---

[20] Mohammed Nader Farhad, "Manage Afghan Labour Migration
to Curb Irregular Flow to Iran, Study Urges," United Nations High
Commissioner for Refugees, 11 December 2008.
[21] Farhad, "Manage Afghan Labour Migration to Curb Irregular
Flow to Iran, Study Urges."
[22] "Mass Deportation from Iran May Cause Crisis, Official Warns,"
New Humanitarian, 27 February 2008.
[23] "Afghan Remittances from Iran Total $500 Million Annually,
Says UN Report," UN News, 7 December 2008.

tions but enlisting in the insurgent's ranks."[24] The news media has reported several cases of young unemployed Afghan men joining the Taliban. When young people are uprooted, jobless, intolerant, alienated, and have few opportunities for positive engagement, they represent a ready pool of recruits for groups seeking to mobilize violence, such as the Taliban and Islamic State of Iraq and Syria (ISIS).[25]

The Total Cost of War in Afghanistan, 2001–20
THE HUMAN COST

According to the Watson Institute for International and Public Affairs at Brown University in Providence, Rhode Island, the total human fatality of the war in Afghanistan has accounted for more than 157,000 deaths since the war began in October 2001.[26] The total number of U.S. servicemembers killed in Afghanistan amounts to 2,314 as of August 2020.[27] The following graph shows the number of U.S. troops killed in action during the execution of Operation Enduring Freedom (OEF) and Operation Freedom's Sentinel (OFS) from

---

[24] *EASO Country of Origin Information Report: Afghanistan Recruitment by Armed Groups* (Luxembourg: Publications Office of the European Union, 2016), 20.

[25] "Poverty Pushing Youth into Arms of Taliban?," *New Humanitarian*, 27 February 2008.

[26] Neta C. Crawford and Catherine Lutz, *Human Cost of Post 9/11 Wars: Direct War Deaths in Major War Zones, Afghanistan and Pakistan (October 2001–October 2019); Iraq (March 2003–October 2019); Syria (September 2014–October 2019); Yemen (October 2002–October 2019); and Other* (Providence, RI: Watson Institute for International and Public Affairs, Brown University, 2019).

[27] "Casualty Status," press release, Department of Defense, 19 July 2021.

Figure 32. U.S. servicemembers killed in Afghanistan, 2001–20

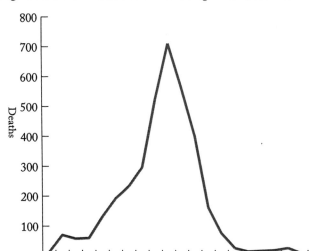

Source: "Number of Fatalities among Western Coalition Soldiers Involved in the Execution of Operation Enduring Freedom from 2001 to 2020," Statista, 2021.

2001 to 2020 (figure 32). As illustrated, the number of casualties steadily increased from 2004 and peaked with the largest number of casualties in a year at 710 in 2010.[28] One of the main reasons for this increase in fatalities was the escalation of the war. The Taliban, once considered defeated in 2001, reemerged as a greater force than anticipated.

In addition to U.S. servicemembers, troops from

[28] "Number of Fatalities among Western Coalition Soldiers Involved in the Execution of Operation Enduring Freedom from 2001 to 2020," Statista, 2021.

Figure 33. International troops killed in Afghanistan, 2001–20

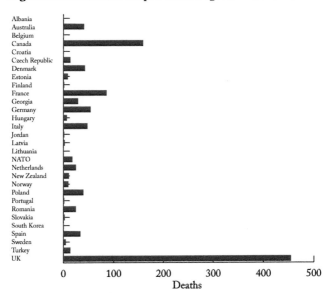

Source: "Number of Fatalities among Western Coalition Soldiers Involved in the Execution of Operation Enduring Freedom from 2001 to 2020," Statista, 2021.

51 other North Atlantic Treaty Organization (NATO) and partner nations in Afghanistan created a Western Coalition during the Global War on Terrorism. They also endured casualties, as described in the chart above (figure 33). Troops from the United Kingdom, Canada, France, and Germany sustained the highest level of casualties after the United States, with 455, 158, 86, and 54 troops killed, respectively.[29]

---

[29] "Number of Fatalities among Western Coalition Soldiers Involved in the Execution of Operation Enduring Freedom from 2001 to 2020."

U.S. and Western Coalition casualties started to decline in 2010 as the Afghan National Security Forces (ANSF) took the lead in the battle with the Taliban. Afghans were now at the forefront of the fight, with the support from the Western Coalition militaries, including the United States. As they took the lead, however, their casualties increased. Since the ANSF had limited training and equipment, their casualties skyrocketed as more action took place. The total number of ANP and ANA deaths is not clear. However, in September 2013, the commander of the International Security Assistance Force (ISAF) in Afghanistan, U.S. Marine Corps general Joseph F. Dunford Jr., said that more than 100 ANSF personnel were being killed each week.[30] In 2014, SIGAR reported 6,785 ANSF killed from January to November 2016, a rate of about 147 per week.[31] In 2016, the Taliban insurgents killed so many Afghan security forces, an average of 22 per day, that the Afghan and U.S. governments agreed to keep battlefield death statistics classified the following year.[32]

Afghan civilians have not been insulated from the dangers of the war; indeed, they have borne the brunt of it. "Almost no civilian in Afghanistan has escaped being personally affected in some way by the ongoing violence," said Tadamichi Yamamoto, the UN Secretary-

---

[30] Emma Graham-Harrison, "Afghan Forces Suffering Too Many Casualties, Says Top NATO Commander," *Guardian*, 2 September 2013.

[31] *Quarterly Report to the United States Congress, Jan 30, 2017* (Arlington, VA: Special Inspector General for Afghanistan Reconstruction, 2017), 98.

[32] Rod Nordland, "The Death Toll for Afghan Forces Is Secret. Here's Why," *New York Times*, 21 September 2018.

General's Special Representative for Afghanistan and head of the UN Assistance Mission in Afghanistan (UNAMA).[33] According to UNAMA, the number of civilian casualties in 2019 had surpassed a grim milestone of 100,000 people killed during the war.[34]

The war also claimed the lives of more than 65 journalists and 400 humanitarian workers.[35] Reporters Without Borders (*Reporters sans Frontières*, RSF) considers Afghanistan one of the deadliest places for journalists to work, with increased fatalities due to bombings and targeted shootings.[36]

THE DOLLAR COST

According to the latest SIGAR report, as of December 2020, the United States appropriated approximately $143.27 billion for Afghanistan reconstruction and $815.7 billion for OEF and OFS in Afghanistan since 2002.[37] In simpler terms, this $143.27 billion spent is considered humanitarian assistance (military and non-military spending) and primarily consisted of obligations of USAID and the U.S. Departments of State and Defense. The $815.7 billion was mainly U.S. military spending, including the cost of maintaining U.S. troops in Afghanistan, conducting counterinsurgency opera-

---

[33] "Afghanistan: Civilian Casualties Exceed 10,000 for Sixth Straight Year," UN News, 22 February 2020.

[34] "Afghanistan: Civilian Casualties Exceed 10,000 for Sixth Straight Year."

[35] Crawford and Lutz, *Human Cost of Post-9/11 Wars*.

[36] "Afghanistan among 'Deadliest Countries' for Reporters: RSF," TOLO News, 21 April 2020.

[37] *Quarterly Report to the United States Congress, Jan 30, 2021* (Arlington, VA: Special Inspector General for Afghanistan Reconstruction, 2021), 28.

tions, and supplying American troops with food, clothing, medical care, special pay, and benefits.

More than $16.90 billion of the $143.27 billion for Afghanistan reconstruction was provided directly in budget assistance to the government of Afghanistan.[38] This included nearly $10.94 billion given to Afghan government ministries and institutions and more than $5.96 billion given to the following multinational trust funds, which supported various projects in coordination with the government of Afghanistan:[39]

- World Bank-managed Afghanistan Reconstruction Trust Fund (ARTF)
- United Nations-managed Law and Order Trust Fund for Afghanistan (LOTFA)
- Asian Development Bank-managed Afghanistan Infrastructure Trust Fund (AITF)

These multilateral institutions played a significant role in supporting Afghanistan relief and reconstruction efforts. In addition to the United States, various other major donors including Japan, the United Kingdom, Germany, the European Union, Canada, Australia, Norway, the Netherlands, and Italy had provided more than $22.7 billion since 2002 for Afghanistan reconstruction efforts (figure 34).[40]

Table 1 puts the overall cost of the international community's nation-building efforts in Afghanistan

---

[38] *Quarterly Report to the United States Congress, Jan 30, 2021*, 27.

[39] *Quarterly Report to the United States Congress, Jan 30, 2021*, 27.

[40] *Quarterly Report to the United States Congress, Jan 30, 2021*.

Figure 34. Contributions to ARTF, UNOCHA, LOTFA, and NATO Afghan National Army programs, 2002–20, USD billions

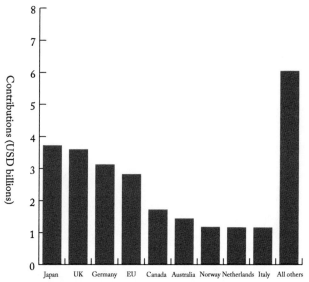

Source: *Quarterly Report to the United States Congress, Jan 30, 2021* (Arlington, VA: Special Inspector General for Afghanistan Reconstruction, 2021).

Table 1. International spending to rebuild Afghanistan, USD billions

U.S. military spending	$815.7 billion
U.S. nonmilitary aid	$53 billion
U.S. military aid	$90.27 billion
International funding	$23 billion
TOTAL	**$981.97 billion**

Source: *Quarterly Report to the United States Congress, Jan 30, 2021* (Arlington, VA: Special Inspector General for Afghanistan Reconstruction, 2021).

into perspective. The total price tag comes to just $18 billion short of $1 trillion during the course of the conflict in Afghanistan.

To further scrutinize the overall price tag of $982 billion, the following graph highlights the percentage of U.S. military and nonmilitary spending in Afghanistan (figure 35).[41] These data points represent a staggering divergence in priorities, unlike what happened in Europe after World War II with the Marshall Plan fund. The U.S. humanitarian aid component of this spending package accounts for approximately $143.27 billion, which is divided into four major categories of reconstruction and related funding: security, governance and development, humanitarian, and oversight and operations. The following chart indicates that of the total $143.27 billion, 64 percent has been spent on security, 26 percent on governance and development, and only 3 percent for humanitarian needs (figure 36).[42]

Under the governance and development category, five distinct programs are important to highlight, primarily because of the disproportionate allocation of money for them. The amount of money assigned to each program is not aligned with the true needs of the Afghan people on the ground. This impracticable approach emphasizes the fact that policymakers in Washington,

---

[41] As shown in figure 35, 83 percent of the overall U.S. expenditures in Afghanistan has had some sort of a military element to it. For example, 9 percent of the total aid has been allocated to Afghan security forces, which also has a large military portion to it. Only 5.4 percent of the nearly $1 trillion spent in Afghanistan so far has been appropriated for humanitarian assistance. *Quarterly Report to the United States Congress, Jan 30, 2021*, 26–45.

[42] *Quarterly Report to the United States Congress, Jan 30, 2021*, 26–45.

Figure 35. Military and nonmilitary resource allocations, 2001–20, percentage

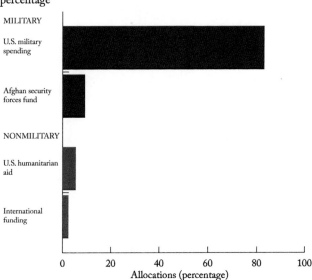

Source: *Quarterly Report to the United States Congress, Jan 30, 2021* (Arlington, VA: Special Inspector General for Afghanistan Reconstruction, 2021).

DC, international development experts in Kabul, and Afghan politicians have failed to understand the basic needs of the population and the disconnect between those managing the funds and those who need the aid.

According to the SIGAR report, the U.S. Agency for Global Media (USAGM), which runs the Voice of America Dari and Pashto language programs and Radio Freedom in Afghanistan, was funded by more than $281 million (USD) in the last 10 years.[43] In compari-

---

[43] *Quarterly Report to the United States Congress, Jan 30, 2021*, 172.

Figure 36. Total aid allocations to Afghanistan, by program, 2001–20, percentage

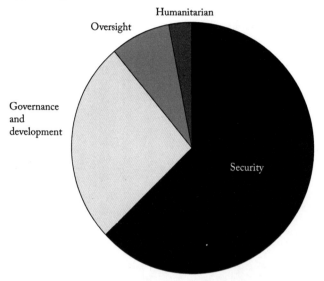

Source: *Quarterly Report to the United States Congress, Jan 30, 2021* (Arlington, VA: Special Inspector General for Afghanistan Reconstruction, 2021).

son, the U.S. Department of State-sponsored exchange programs, such as the Fulbright Foreign Student Program and Youth Exchange and Study (YES) Program, which supported the author's education in the United States, only received $96.5 million in the last 20 year (figure 37).[44] The funding for these exchange programs has continued to decrease in recent years mainly due to the cancellation of the YES Program in 2012, which had been bringing in more than 40 high school ex-

---

[44] *Quarterly Report to the United States Congress, Jan 30, 2021*, 172.

Figure 37. Education compared with USAGM funding allocations, 2009–20, USD millions

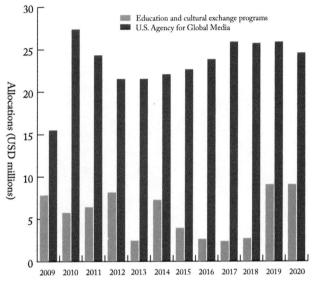

Source: *Quarterly Report to the United States Congress, Jan 30, 2021* (Arlington, VA: Special Inspector General for Afghanistan Reconstruction, 2021).

change students from across Afghanistan to the United States for one school year. It could be argued that public awareness through USAGM is more critical than the educational exchange programs, given that educational programs such as YES and Fulbright have already done a lot more for cultural awareness and cross-culture pollination than any media awareness campaign could. However, the importance of these exchange programs in building the capacity of Afghan youth who are currently playing a vital role in the Afghan government and may become future leaders in the country cannot be measured. Having a cadre of people who can fill future leadership roles in the government would not only help with effective governance but also extend the benefit of peace and prosperity across the region and throughout the world. Hence, these funds have not been focused on the most efficient use.

When comparing funding for youth survival and health with the International Narcotics Control and Law Enforcement (INCLE) program, data shows that for every $100 spent on the INCLE program, child health programs received only $9 in the last two decades (figure 38). At the same time, according to a recent UN report, "there are two million children in [Afghanistan] which suffer from acute malnutrition, among them 600,000 children that suffer from severe acute malnutrition."[45] Also, according to the British Broadcasting Corporation (BBC), the United States has spent on average $1.5 million a day since 2002, or nearly $9 billion, on antinarcotics efforts.[46] Yet, UN figures show that the total estimated area devoted to opium poppy cultivation reached a record high in 2017.[47] The White House Office of National Drug Control Policy report issued in February 2020 indicated that the highest level of opi-

---

[45] Approximately 600,000 Afghan children face death through malnutrition without emergency funds. See "Two Million Children under Five Suffering from Acute Malnutrition in Afghanistan," press release, UNICEF, accessed 10 September 2021.

[46] Justin Rowlatt, "How the US Military's Opium War in Afghanistan Was Lost," BBC News, 25 April 2019.

[47] "Record-high Opium Production in Afghanistan Creates Multiple Challenges for Region and Beyond, UN Warns," UN News, 21 May 2018.

Figure 38. Child health program compared with narcotics control program fund allocations, 2009–20, USD millions

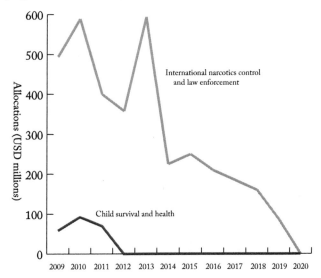

Source: *Quarterly Report to the United States Congress, Jan 30, 2021* (Arlington, VA: Special Inspector General for Afghanistan Reconstruction, 2021).

um was produced in 2017 with 9,140 metric tons, and 2019 was the second-highest year for poppy cultivation in that count.[48]

Moreover, Afghanistan's infrastructure was severely crippled due to the decades of war and has only received a small fraction of the total aid directed to the United States' reconstruction efforts in that country. Accord-

---

[48] Phillip Walter Wellman, "White House: Afghanistan Opium Yield Expected to Rise Even as Acreage Planted to Poppies Falls," *Stars and Stripes*, 10 February 2020.

Figure 39. Afghanistan Infrastructure Trust Fund allocations, 2009–20, USD millions

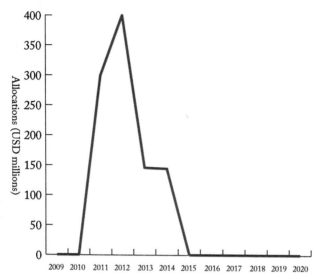

Source: *Quarterly Report to the United States Congress, Jan 30, 2021* (Arlington, VA: Special Inspector General for Afghanistan Reconstruction, 2021).

ing to the SIGAR report, the Afghanistan Infrastructure Trust Fund, which provides significant funding to support Afghanistan relief and reconstruction efforts through multilateral institutions like the Asian Development Bank and the World Bank, has only received 2.82 percent of the total aid money given to Afghanistan, and that funding ceased in the last five years (figure 39). The United States' major contribution to the fund came during 2011–14.[49] Nonetheless, Kabul, Afghani-

---

[49] *Quarterly Report to the United States Congress, Jan 30, 2021*, 172.

stan's capital city, remains without regular electricity due to a lack of funding and infrastructure insecurity. Despite the fact that billions of dollars have been poured into reconstruction efforts, Afghans continue to suffer from a lack of basic infrastructure needs, such as roads, bridges, and tunnels, which are required to help the nascent market economy flourish.[50]

---

[50] Dante Schultz, "The Urgent Need to Expand Afghanistan's Electricity Supplies," Caspian Policy Center, 29 January 2021.

CHAPTER SIX

Legitimizing the Taliban

The Surrender-to-the-Taliban Strategy

Prior to becoming president, Donald J. Trump had extensively criticized the United States' involvement in Afghanistan. He stated that invading Afghanistan in 2001 was a "bad mistake." He began pushing for an end to the conflict in Afghanistan as early as 2011. In one of his tweets, Trump called Afghanistan "a complete waste." Furthermore, he added that it was "time to come home!" In yet another tweet, he claimed that the United States had "wasted an enormous amount of blood and treasure . . . wasted lives" in Afghanistan. He called the war "nonsense" and called for the rebuilding of America instead.[1]

Despite this early rhetoric, Afghanistan was barely mentioned by the candidates during the 2016 presidential campaign. The GOP platform was noticeably quiet on the topic. Trump was asked whether he thought "American boots should continue on the ground in Afghanistan" during an interview with CNN in October 2015. "We made a terrible mistake getting involved there in the first place," Trump said. "It's a mess, it's a mess and at this point we probably have to (leave U.S. troops in Afghanistan) because that thing will collapse in about two seconds after they leave." He did, however,

---

[1] Jon Schwarz and Robert Mackey, "All the Times Donald Trump Said the U.S. Should Get Out of Afghanistan," Intercept, 21 August 2017.

later qualify his comments: "I would leave the troops there, begrudgingly."[2]

Following his election, and after months of deliberation and discussions with various stakeholders, including the government of Afghanistan, President Trump delivered his "strategy in Afghanistan and South Asia" in August 2017. He started by acknowledging that the U.S. war in Afghanistan was the longest war in American history. "I share the American people's frustration," he added. "I also share their frustration over a foreign policy that has spent too much time, energy, money and most importantly lives, trying to rebuild countries in our own image, instead of pursuing our security interests above all other considerations."[3]

Trump's strategy for Afghanistan was based on the following three pillars:

1. A plan of victory for those in combat. "They deserve the tools they need, and the trust they have earned, to fight and to win," Trump said in his speech.[4] Despite his original instinct, which was to pull out of Afghanistan completely, he thought the consequences of a rapid exit would be both predictable and unacceptable. A hasty withdrawal would create a vacuum that terrorists, includ-

---

[2] Jeremy Diamond, "Donald Trump: Afghanistan War a 'Mistake,' but Troops Need to Stay," CNN, 6 October 2015.

[3] Donald J. Trump, "Remarks by President Trump on the Strategy in Afghanistan and South Asia" (speech, Fort Myer, Arlington, VA, 21 August 2017), hereafter Trump remarks.

[4] Trump remarks.

ing the Islamic State of Iraq and Syria (ISIS) and al-Qaeda, would fill, as witnessed in Iraq in 2011.[5]

2. A plan that would not repeat the same mistakes made in Iraq. A core pillar of the new U.S. strategy was to shift from a time-based approach to one based on conditions. "Conditions on the ground—not arbitrary timetables—will guide our strategy from now on," the president said.[6]

3. A plan that would use all the United States' diplomatic, economic, and military might to achieve a successful outcome in Afghanistan. This included negotiating a political settlement with the Taliban.

Trump vowed that the United States is not "nation-building again" but "killing terrorists" in Afghanistan. "However," the president's strategy concluded, "our commitment [to Afghanistan] is not unlimited, and our support is not a blank check. The government of Afghanistan must carry their share of the military, political, and economic burden."[7]

The term *blank check* was used by U.S. president Barack H. Obama in his strategy for Afghanistan as

---

[5] Trump remarks.

[6] Trump remarks.

[7] Trump remarks.

well.[8] The pattern here is quite interesting, in which both a Democratic and Republican president did not trust the government of Afghanistan. Both believed that American taxpayer dollars were being squandered in that country.

Trump's decision for the United States to keep boots on the ground with a somewhat enlarged military presence is what the Afghan people wanted. However, the president's approach contained two critical and fundamental flaws. First, the Trump administration sidelined the Afghan government in most, if not all, of its decisions regarding Afghanistan. Second, it reduced development aid to historical lows.[9]

The government of Afghanistan was shut out of U.S.–Taliban peace talks in Qatar. They were not privy to the closed-door negotiations taking place between U.S. Special Representative for Afghanistan Reconciliation Zalmay M. Khalilzad and the Taliban on a peace deal. President of Afghanistan Ashraf Ghani was so frustrated that he lashed out at U.S. officials through his national security advisor, Hamdullah Mohib, who said a U.S.–Taliban deal would dishonor fallen U.S. troops and called Khalilzad an American "viceroy" with ambitions to head an interim Afghan government.[10] The comments became so heated that the U.S. Depart-

[8] Barack H. Obama, "Remarks by the President on a New Strategy for Afghanistan and Pakistan" (speech, Dwight D. Eisenhower Executive Office Building, Washington, DC, 27 March 2009).

[9] Conor Finnegan, "US Signs Historic Deal with Taliban, Trump Announces, Beginning End of US War in Afghanistan and Withdrawal of American Troops," ABC News, 29 February 2020.

[10] Rod Nordland and Mujib Mashal, "Afghan National Security Chief Is Sidelined in His Own War," *New York Times*, 30 March 2019.

ment of State summoned Mohib and warned him that his comments could hurt bilateral relations in the peace process.[11]

In 2020, the Afghan government was caught by surprise when Trump announced on Twitter that the last of the U.S. troops in Afghanistan would return home before the end of December. The tweet contradicted remarks by his national security advisor, Robert C. O'Brien Jr., who said that "as of today, there are under 5,000 [U.S. troops in Afghanistan] and that will go down to 2,500 by early next year."[12] Taliban spokesman Zabihullah Mujahed welcomed Trump's statement and called it a positive step for the peace agreement.[13]

Economic Development Assistance during the Trump Era

President Donald Trump's "America first" policy was based on the concept of retreating from America's intervention abroad, including drastically cutting foreign aid. In his 2017 budget proposal, one thing was evident when Trump announced in May: "America First" meant less money for foreign aid. The president wanted to cut foreign aid by up to 37 percent, and there were rumors that some administration officials were considering merging USAID and the Department of State.[14]

---

[11] Craig Nelson, "U.S. Officials Walk Out of Meeting at Presidential Palace in Kabul," *Wall Street Journal*, 26 March 2019.

[12] Kathy Gannon, "Taliban Cheer Trump Tweet Promising Early Troop Withdrawal," ABC News, 8 October 2020.

[13] Lolita C. Baldor and Kathy Gannon, "Military Blindsided by Trump's New Afghan Troop Withdrawal," AP News, 8 October 2020.

[14] Molli Ferrarello, "What 'America First' Means for US Foreign Aid," *Brookings Now* (blog), Brookings, 27 July 2017.

For the general public, there are misconceptions about U.S. spending on foreign assistance. While public opinion polls show that Americans believe that foreign aid accounts for around 25 percent of federal spending, it actually accounts for less than 1 percent of the federal budget. Another fallacy is that foreign aid is unpopular in the United States. According to polling conducted during the last 25 years, up to 75 percent of Americans support international aid initiatives.[15] In this process, development aid to Afghanistan also came under the chopping block of the Trump administration. On the economic development front, President Trump's administration cut back on aid to Afghanistan significantly from 2017 through 2019. According to USAID, on average about $2.4 billion in assistance was appropriated for Afghanistan development during this period (figure 40).[16]

This massive reduction in American aid to the war-ravaged and poverty-ridden country could not have come at a more difficult time as COVID-19 battered the local Afghan economy. When COVID struck in early spring 2020, Afghanistan was already in the midst of a prolonged conflict, an uncertain political climate, and a tenuous peace process.[17] In March, the

---

[15] George Ingram, "Myths about U.S. Foreign Aid," *Unpacked* (blog), Brookings, 7 April 2017.

[16] In comparison, the Obama administration sent more than $9.5 billion on average per year during its tenure. Figure 40 highlights 2019 as the year with the lowest amount of U.S. assistance to Afghanistan since the war began in 2001, with only $345 million. "Foreign Aid Explorer," USAID, 2021.

[17] *Afghanistan Study Group Final Report, February 2021* (Washington, DC: U.S. Institute of Peace, 2021).

Figure 40. A comparison of Trump-era aid to Afghanistan, 2001–19, USD millions

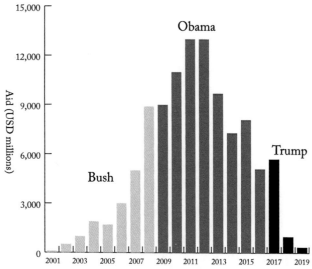

Source: "Foreign Aid Explorer," USAID, 2021.

government-imposed restrictions forced many day-laborers further into poverty and hunger.[18] According to the most recent household survey, nearly 15 million Afghans in 2 million households are vulnerable to economic lockdown.[19] Most of these people earn their living from activities such as shop keeping, selling groceries, selling fruit on a pushcart, or physical day labor.

---

[18] Stefanie Glinski, " 'No Profit, No Food': Lockdown in Kabul Prompts Hunger Fears," *Guardian*, 1 April 2020.

[19] Cesar A. Cancho and Tejesh Pradhan, "Mitigating the Poverty Implications of COVID-19 in Afghanistan," *End Poverty in South Asia* (blog), World Bank, 16 August 2020.

Without a reliable stream of income, some of these people had to sell their belongings to feed their families.[20]

According to a recent World Bank publication, COVID lockdowns and restrictions will result in heightened poverty across Afghanistan. By some estimates, one in every five households will see their income decline by 75 percent or more due to COVID shock. Overall, Afghanistan's economy is set to contract by 7.4 percent in 2020 because of COVID, exacerbating poverty and leading to a sharp decline in government revenues. World Bank estimates show the poverty rate increasing from a baseline of 54.5 percent in 2017 to up to 72 percent in 2020.[21] According to a recent Asian Development Bank report, the fiscal revenue of Afghanistan fell in 2020 due to the pandemic from approximately 13.6 percent of GDP in 2019 to about 15 percent in 2020. Exports declined by more than 28 percent in the second half of 2020.[22]

Amid the pandemic and rising food insecurity, inflation is yet another major concern. Afghanistan is an import-driven economy, with more than 80 percent of its food imported from neighboring countries. COVID lockdowns have resulted in global food price increases, including in Afghanistan. Before the pandemic, the price of a bag of flour was about $19 (USD). Within a week, the price of the same bag increased by 31 percent

---

[20] Cancho and Pradhan, "Mitigating the Poverty Implications of COVID-19 in Afghanistan."

[21] Cancho and Pradhan, "Mitigating the Poverty Implications of COVID-19 in Afghanistan."

[22] Mir Haidar Shah Omid, "ADB Predicts Decline in Afghanistan's Economic Growth," TOLO News, 15 September 2020.

to about $25, leaving some people without bread—a vital nutritional supplement on every Afghan dining table.[23] However, inflation is projected to moderate to 5 percent in 2021 and 4 percent in 2022 as food supplies improve.[24]

The Peace Deal with the Taliban

Despite other challenges, the Afghan government and the Trump administration had been mostly focused on striking a peace deal with the Taliban. While people were suffering from hunger and economic devastation, the highest priority for the two governments continued to be peace talks with the group that has killed hundreds of thousands of Afghans and Americans. At one point, Trump considered inviting the Taliban leaders to Camp David, Maryland, in September 2019. Talks broke down and the invitation was withdrawn after the Taliban killed an American soldier and 12 other people in Kabul.[25] Peace negotiations were called off for some period thereafter. However, after an 18-month negotiation process, the United States ultimately signed a peace deal with the Taliban in Doha, Qatar, in February 2020.[26] The peace deal reached to end the 19-year-long Afghan conflict marked the beginning of a phased

---

[23] Stephanie Glinski, "Food Prices Soar under Coronavirus Threat in Afghanistan," *New Humanitarian*, 7 April 2020.

[24] *Afghanistan's Economy to Rebound in 2021 Despite Challenges* (Manila, Philippines: Asian Development Bank, 2021).

[25] Jonathan Lemire and Deb Reichmann, "Trump Calls Off Secret Meeting with Taliban, Afghan Leaders," AP News, 7 September 2019.

[26] Lindsay Maizland, "U.S.-Taliban Peace Deal: What to Know," Council on Foreign Relations, 2 March 2020.

withdrawal of American soldiers from the South Asian country. At the start of 2020, the United States had fewer than 13,000 troops in Afghanistan. However, after signing the deal with the Taliban, that number dropped substantially, and by January 2021, only about 2,500 U.S. troops were left in Afghanistan.[27]

The agreement had the following four points:

1. The United States and the North Atlantic Treaty Organization (NATO) must withdraw all their troops from Afghanistan within 14 months. While the majority of Afghans support the U.S. presence in their country, a small infringed minority—the Taliban—were now calling the shots in Afghanistan and its future.

2. The Taliban must guarantee that Afghan soil will not be used as a launchpad that would threaten the security of the United States. Islamic State of Iraq and the Levant–Khorasan Province (ISIS–K) and various other local militia groups are active in Afghanistan using the platform provided by the Taliban.[28] It is extremely difficult for the Taliban to ensure that these groups re-

[27] Ayaz Gul, "Pompeo Defends Trump's Afghan Peace Plan, Ensuing 'Incredible Progress'," VOA News, 2 January 2021.

[28] ISIS–K refers to a branch of the militant Islamist group ISIS that is active in South Asia and Central Asia. See Paul Lushenko, Lance Van Auken, and Garrett Stebbins, "ISIS–K: Deadly Nuisance or Strategic Threat?," *Small Wars & Insurgencies* 30, no. 2 (2019): 265–78, https://doi.org/10.1080/09592318.2018.1546293.

main committed to the deal they made with the United States. While ISIS–K and other groups are poised and unified around the cause to fight the U.S. and Afghan governments, the Taliban leadership is fragmented at best and adversarial at worst.

3. The Taliban must negotiate with the government of Afghanistan on a power-sharing deal. H. R. McMaster, President Trump's former national security advisor, recently said in an interview: "What (does) power-sharing with the Taliban look like? Does that look like . . . every other girls' school bulldozed? Or does it look like mass executions in the soccer stadium every other Saturday?"[29] The question remains: What would this power-sharing deal with the Taliban look like? How much of the recent gains in terms of women's empowerment, economic development, and social liberties would Afghans have to sacrifice?

4. A permanent and comprehensive ceasefire must be achieved. Since the United States signed the so-called peace deal with the Taliban, the war against Afghan soldiers and its po-

---

[29] Deirdre Shesgreen, "Trump's Ex-national Security Adviser H. R. McMaster Warns Afghan Peace Talks Will Fail, Leave US Vulnerable," *USA Today*, 21 September 2020.

lice force significantly intensified. The United States and Taliban struck a truce, but there was no ceasefire in sight for Afghans.

As a direct result of the deal with the United States, the Taliban ceased their attacks on foreign troops. No U.S. servicemembers were killed in Afghanistan for more than a year since the Trump 2020 deal was struck.[30] However, the Taliban increased their offensive against the Afghan National Army (ANA), the Afghan National Police (ANP), and ordinary Afghans. According to the *New York Times*, "at least 703 Afghan security forces and 208 civilians were killed . . . in June [alone], the highest count among security forces since . . . September 2018."[31] Afghan civilian casualties increased 29 percent during the first three months of 2021, according to a UN report.[32]

In January 2021, when President Joseph R. Biden Jr. came into office, he was now the fourth U.S. president—two Republicans and two Democrats—to preside over this prolonged war. As with his predecessors, the Afghan war was one of the foreign policy challenges handed to him, and he had to decide how to deal with it. Biden's options were to either support the so-called "Trump-deal" with the Taliban or change course. Biden took his time to review the Afghanistan policy for the

---

[30] Gul, "Pompeo Defends Trump's Afghan Peace Plan, Ensuing 'Incredible Progress'."

[31] "Afghan War Casualty Report: June 2021," *New York Times*, 4 August 2021.

[32] Ayaz Gul, "Afghan Civilian Casualties Spiked 29%, UN Reports," VOA News, 14 April 2021.

first several months in office. On 14 April, he announced his administration's approach to the war. He delivered his strategy from the Treaty Room at the White House, the same location where President George W. Bush announced the start of the war on 7 October 2001, and called for an end to America's longest war.[33] While he offered few specifics about his approach to the war during the 2020 presidential campaign, Afghans and those involved in Afghanistan affairs had a good sense as to where candidate Biden stood on this issue. As President Barack H. Obama's vice president in 2009, Biden was one of the few voices in the administration who advised the president to lean toward a smaller counterterrorism role in Afghanistan.[34] He argued for a residual force of about 2,500 troops that would only conduct surveillance and over-the-horizon operations to go after high-risk Taliban and al-Qaeda figures.[35]

Now as president, Biden wanted to deliver on what he had previously argued was the right approach for the war in Afghanistan. First, he outlined the reason for America's continued involvement in the war, which he believed was "to ensure that Afghanistan would not be used as a base from which to attack our homeland again." He argued that the United States had accomplished that goal. Second, Osama bin Laden, master-

---

[33] Aamer Madhani and Matthew Lee, "Biden to Pull US Troops from Afghanistan, End 'Forever War'," AP News, 14 April 2021.

[34] Max Fisher, "In White House, Biden Pushes Back on Afghanistan," *Atlantic*, 14 October 2009.

[35] *Over-the-horizon* refers to an operation launched from beyond the visual and radar range of the area. Carol E. Lee, "Frustrated Military Officials Want Biden to Make a Decision on Afghanistan," NBC News, 8 April 2021.

mind of the 9/11 attacks, had been killed, so the reasons for remaining in Afghanistan were becoming increasingly unclear. Therefore, Biden decided to end America's longest war by bringing all American troops out of Afghanistan by 31 August 2021 with no conditions attached, four months later than the 1 May deadline originally set by the Trump administration.[36]

In his approach, President Biden had significantly overestimated the Afghan government's capacity. Presumably, he was confident that a government backed by the United States for more than two decades could now stand on its feet as the American presence diminished. In July 2021, when asked by a reporter whether he had confidence that the Afghan government would not collapse after full U.S. withdrawal, Biden said, "[The Afghan government] clearly [has] the capacity to sustain the government in place. They have the forces. They have the equipment. . . . The likelihood there's going to be the Taliban overrunning everything and owning the whole country is highly unlikely."[37]

He could not have been more wrong. As Biden announced the U.S. withdrawal from Afghanistan without any preconditions, the Taliban gained momentum and began their massive offensive against the Afghan government. The United States lost any considerable leverage over the Taliban by announcing that we would withdraw regardless and with no conditions attached.

---

[36] Joseph R. Biden, "Remarks by President Biden on the Way Forward in Afghanistan" (speech, Treaty Room, White House, 14 April 2021).

[37] Joseph R. Biden, "Remarks by President Biden on the Drawdown of U.S. Forces in Afghanistan" (speech, East Room, White House, 8 July 2021).

The Taliban now had no one to fear or hide from, but could now fight the nascent ANA and ANP that were grappling with the new reality of no foreign troop support. The Taliban considered themselves victorious—a small group that defeated a superpower. Their foot soldiers gained confidence as their leadership gained an upper hand in the talks with the Afghan government in Doha, Qatar. Their negotiating team no longer seemed interested in discussing the establishment of an inclusive government with the Ashraf Ghani administration. They had their eye on the prize, which was closer than they had previously expected.[38]

Until 5 August 2021, the central government of Afghanistan had control over all the provincial capitals of 34 provinces, according to the *Long War Journal*. A day later, the Taliban captured two provincial capitals: Zaranj, the capital of Nimroz Province; and Sar-e Pol the capital of Sar-e Pol Province. Five days later, on 12 August, one of the largest provinces, Herat, fell to the Taliban, and Kandahar then fell the following day.[39] On 15 August, people in Kabul woke up to an ordinary day and went about their daily activities, until it was announced later that afternoon that President Ghani had fled the country.[40] Reports indicated that everyone in the government, including the security forces, aban-

---

[38] Diaa Hadid, "U.S. Unconditional Withdrawal Rattles Afghanistan's Shaky Peace Talks," NPR, 29 April 2021.

[39] Bill Roggio, "Mapping Taliban Control in Afghanistan," *Long War Journal*, accessed 10 September 2021.

[40] "Afghan President Says He Left Country to Avoid Bloodshed," Reuters, 15 August 2021.

doned their posts as the news spread.[41] Afghans were now left to the mercy of a brutal force, the Taliban. Utter chaos and panic erupted on the streets of Kabul as the day wore on. At the airport, a desperate exodus was taking place, with thousands of people clamoring to board flights. By the evening, scenes of the Taliban entering the presidential palace and posing with guns and rifles in Ashraf Ghani's lavish presidential office emerged. Utter shock and mayhem consumed the capital city, which was now in full control of the Taliban. The government that the United States had propped up for two decades with massive of amounts of blood and money collapsed within 11 days.[42]

The rapidly evolving situation caught many by surprise, including the U.S. government and the Taliban.[43] "We've seen that that [Afghan] force has been unable to defend the country, and that [the collapse of the Afghan government] has happened more quickly than we anticipated," Secretary of State Antony J. Blinken told CNN.[44] The Biden administration quickly announced a massive evacuation operation by sending 6,000 troops back to Kabul to facilitate the process. The 31 August deadline for a full withdrawal of servicemembers was

[41] Clarissa Ward et al., "Afghan President Ashraf Ghani Flees the Country as Taliban Forces Enter the Capital," CNN, 16 August 2021.
[42] Mary Walsh, "11 Days in August: How Afghanistan Fell," CBS News, 22 August 2021.
[43] Ahmed Mengli et al., "Afghan President Flees Country as U.S. Rushes to Exit with Taliban on Brink of Power," NBC News, 15 August 2021.
[44] "Secretary Antony J. Blinken with Jake Tapper of State of the Union on CNN," press release, U.S. Department of State, 15 August 2021.

looming large as the Pentagon initiated the evacuation of Americans and their Afghan staffers who had helped with the 20-year-long war. As the Americans scrambled to depart, the Afghans were left in shock. The Taliban leadership began their victorious chants by releasing a video congratulating everyone for their success. Abdul Ghani Baradar said in a recorded video from Doha: "We have reached a victory that wasn't expected."[45] They began taking charge of the city by sending group chat messages via WhatsApp and Facebook, proclaiming that the Islamic Emirate was now in charge of security in Kabul. The messages listed phone numbers for citizens to call if they saw problems such as looting or armed robbery.[46]

The Pentagon and the Department of State completed a chaotic evacuation and a total troop pullout by 31 August. Once the operation began on 14 August, the United States was able to evacuate more than 116,700 people from Afghanistan, including 5,500 U.S. citizens and their families.[47] During the process, 13 U.S. military personnel and more than 175 Afghans were killed by a suicide attack at the crowded entrance of the Kabul International Airport.[48] U.S. Army major general Christopher T. Donahue was the last Ameri-

---

[45] Susannah George et al., "Afghan Government Collapses as Taliban Sweeps in, U.S. Sends More Troops to Aid Chaotic Withdrawal," *Washington Post*, 15 August 2021.

[46] George et al., "Afghan Government Collapses as Taliban Sweeps in, U.S. Sends More Troops to Aid Chaotic Withdrawal."

[47] Amanda Macias, "U.S. Winds Down Kabul Mission after Helping Evacuate 116,000 People in Just over 2 Weeks," CNBC, 30 August 2021.

[48] "US Says Drone Kills Suicide Bombers Targeting Kabul Airport," Al Jazeera, 29 August 2021.

can servicemember to leave Afghanistan at midnight 31 August.[49]

The Trump-Biden strategy for Afghanistan was disastrous on multiple fronts for both the United States and Afghanistan. According to John Bolton, former Trump national security advisor, one of the major blunders the Trump negotiators made initially was to sideline the duly elected government of Afghanistan—the Ashraf Ghani administration—when negotiating with the Taliban. Bolton added that "there are a lot of mistakes in the deal [with the Taliban] itself. But the fundamental problem of dealing with this terrorist organization is that the Trump negotiators delegitimized the Afghan government. The government we set up. The government with which all the many flaws had at least some democratic legitimacy, of which Taliban had none."[50]

Many wonder how and why the Afghan National Army collapsed so quickly in those 11 days. Some argue, including President Biden, that they did not have the will to fight. Biden said in a mid-August speech that "American troops cannot and should not be fighting in a war and dying in a war that Afghan forces are not willing to fight for themselves. The Afghan military collapsed, sometimes without trying to fight."[51] In point of fact, the Afghan Army did put up a fight against the

---

[49] "Leaving Afghanistan, U.S. General's Ghostly Image Books Place in History," Reuters, 31 August 2021.

[50] Rudy Takala, "John Bolton Blames Trump for Afghanistan: 'Negotiators Delegitimized the Afghan Government'," Mediaite, 27 August 2021.

[51] Joseph R. Biden, "Remarks by President Biden on Afghanistan" (speech, East Room, White House, 16 August 2021).

Taliban and endured significant losses in recent months and years since the U.S. retreated from their combat role in 2014. More than 66,000 members of the Afghan National Army and Police lost their lives in the last 20 years, while only 2,448 American servicemembers were killed during this same period.[52] The Trump-Biden policy, along with the incompetent political leadership in Kabul, failed to support those who were fighting in the battle. Bolton argued that

> by de-recognizing the government [of Afghanistan during the negotiations with the Taliban] in effect, we [the United States] shattered the morale of the Afghan army. The army is saying well, if the Americans won't even protect that government, why are we going to end up protecting it? That's why honestly, nobody should have been surprised that the army collapsed so quickly when Biden announced the final withdrawal.[53]

In addition, the Trump agreement with the Taliban required the Ashraf Ghani government to release 5,000 Taliban who were imprisoned by the government. Zalmay Khalilzad, the U.S. special representative for Afghanistan reconciliation, pressured the Afghan government last year to release the prisoners as an incentive for the Taliban to make peace. According to H. R. McMaster, "the Taliban viewed the release as a sign of

---

[52] Ellen Knickmeyer, "Costs of the Afghanistan War, in Lives and Dollars," AP News, 17 August 2021.

[53] Takala, "John Bolton Blames Trump for Afghanistan."

weakness and an opportunity to replenish its forces in anticipation of its offensive."[54] Ashraf Ghani half-heartedly agreed to the prisoner release as the pressure from the Trump administration mounted, hoping that it would pave the way for a peaceful settlement with the Taliban.[55] Five months after their release, more than 600 of the released Taliban prisoners were arrested on the battlefield for plotting deadly attacks against government forces and civilians.[56]

However, the Trump agreement with the Taliban did require all U.S. and NATO troops to stage a "conditions-based" complete withdrawal from Afghanistan by May 2021.[57] The conditions-based provision is significant in this case, given that the Biden administration did not abide by the terms:

1. A negotiated political power-sharing deal with the Afghan government
2. A permanent and comprehensive ceasefire must be achieved[58]

The Biden administration called for a full U.S. and NATO troops pullout without achieving either of the aforementioned conditions set in the Trump deal. That alone caused the confidence of the Afghan govern-

[54] H. R. McMaster and Bradley Bowman, "In Afghanistan, the Tragic Toll of Washington Delusion," *Wall Street Journal*, 15 August 2021.

[55] David Welna, "In Reversal, Afghan Leader Agrees to Release Taliban Prisoners," NPR, 11 March 2020.

[56] Ayaz Gul, "Afghan Official: 600 Freed Taliban Prisoners Rearrested," VOA News, 24 January 2021.

[57] Gul, "Afghan Official."

[58] Matthew Lee and Eric Tucker, "Was Biden Handcuffed by Trump's Taliban Deal in Doha?," AP News, 19 August 2021.

ment and security forces to erode as the Taliban pushed through their massive spring offensive against Afghan forces. H. R. McMaster said recently that "we delivered really tremendous psychological blows to the Afghan people, Afghan leaders and Afghan security forces on our way out."[59] The final result was the unexpected collapse of a government in which the United States, along with its NATO allies, heavily invested their lives and money for the last 20 years.

Initially, the Trump administration made the mistake of recognizing the Taliban and giving them legitimacy by engaging with them directly. This action gave the Taliban a platform where their officials could easily operate internationally, traveling on formal visits to various countries including Russia, China, and Iran to seek their support.[60] This legitimacy and freedom of movement created an image of the Taliban around the world in which they propagated this falsehood and claimed that they were no longer the Taliban of the 1990s. It put the Ghani administration in an odd situation and a weakened position.

On the domestic front, Ashraf Ghani failed to build consensus among the political leaders in the country. Electoral tensions during the 2019 presidential campaign grew so heated that the disputed election results caused both Ghani and Abdullah Abdullah, the two top contenders, to hold separate inaugurations on the same

---

[59] "Taliban Takeover of Afghanistan Is an 'American Catastrophe,' H. R. McMaster Says," PBS News Hour, 16 August 2021.
[60] Nilofar Sakhi, "How Russia, China, and Iran Will Shape Afghanistan's Future," *New Atlanticist* (blog), Atlantic Council, 18 June 2021.

day.[61] At the same time, intra-Afghan negotiations with the Taliban were shaping up, and the Afghan government needed to project a strong united front to the Taliban. However, talks were stalled by both sides for months, and negotiation teams made little progress in Doha.[62] The Taliban took advantage of the opportunity and went on a diplomatic blitz in the last year. Their negotiating team traveled to Iran, Pakistan, Turkey, Russia, and later to China on an offensive to seek their support. These visits further legitimized their existence on the Afghan political landscape.

The United States is now seen to have failed miserably in Afghanistan by Afghans and others in the region. NATO allies are rethinking their future defense without the United States. The high representative of the Europena Union for foreign affairs and security policy, Josep Borrell, said "This [the U.S. withdrawal] has been above all a catastrophe for the Afghan people. It's a failure of the Western world and it's a game changer for international relations." Afghanistan has proven just how many allies rely on the United States. As a result, the question of whether Europeans should now wean themselves of that reliance and invest in and build their own security has emerged. During Donald Trump's presidency, French president Emmanuel Macron advocated for a "European army," and events in Afghanistan are reviving a similar debate. Borrell also suggested that

---

[61] "Ghani Takes the Oath of Afghan President. His Rival Does, Too," *New York Times*, 9 March 2020.

[62] "High-stakes Talks between Afghan Gov't, Taliban as Fighting Rages," Al Jazeera, 17 July 2021.

"the EU must be able to intervene to protect our interests when the Americans don't want to be involved."[63]

Conversely, while the Taliban consider themselves victorious and a force to be reckoned with, Afghans have lost everything. They lost the gains made in the past 20 years in a matter of days. Young girls who had never lived under the former Taliban regime are now young adults who aspired to become doctors or teachers. Afghan women who had worked tirelessly and studied hard in hopes of achieving higher goals in life now have no hope to see them to fruition. An Afghan girls' robotics team had the prospect of competing in major international competitions, inventing new tools; however, they were evacuated from Kabul a day after the Taliban took over and now live as refugees in Mexico.[64] In addition, during the last 20 years, hundreds of thousands of Afghan students studied abroad, gained tangible experiences, and returned with the energy and confidence to help develop their country. The human capital deficit that the country had experienced was slowly dissipating. Now, all those young professionals marched en masse with their young children to the Kabul International Airport following the Taliban takeover. Most of the young and educated have either fled the country or intend to leave at the first opportunity. As a result of the loss of the intellectual power of this younger generation, the country will remain impover-

---

[63] Jen Kirby, "NATO Allies Are Preparing for a Future without America's 'Forever Wars'," Vox, 31 August 2021.

[64] Katanga Johnson and Anthony Esposito, "Afghan All-girl Robotics Team Members, Journalists Land in Mexico," Reuters, 25 August 2021.

ished and the cycle of poverty will continue. Those with the means will take refuge in other countries and those without will endure the Taliban's cruelty and economic difficulties for decades to come.

The United States government has lost any influence over the Taliban. Economic sanctions are the only tools left for America and its allies to hold them accountable for their actions. The Taliban 2.0 that was presented to the world in the last year are no different than the Taliban 1.0 of the 1990s. They recently announced a ban on music in public places, claiming that it is forbidden in Islam.[65] As they set up their government, the Taliban announced that no women will fill any cabinet-level positions.[66] Recently, Abdul Baqi Haqqani, the acting higher education minister for the Taliban, announced that girls and boys will no longer be allowed to study in one classroom.[67] There is growing concern that the Taliban would return to their cruel treatment of women and girls, which was prevalent when the militant group controlled the country previously. For the United States and others to vouch for women's rights or any other causes in the country, they would have to use economic aid or sanctions as a leverage against the Taliban. Both these actions would have a significant effect on ordinary Afghans who are already living in a dire economic situation. According to the World Food Programme,

---

[65] Kamal Joshi, "Afghanistan: Taliban Announces Ban on Music in Public Places, Claims 'Forbidden in Islam'," *Republic World*, 26 August 2021.

[66] Roland Oliphant, "Women Will Not Work at Ministerial Level in Taliban Government," *Telegraph*, 1 September 2021.

[67] Mychael Schnell, "Taliban Acting Education Minister Says Mixed Gender University Classes Will Be Banned," *Hill*, 30 August 2021.

Afghanistan is on the verge of a humanitarian crisis. One in three people go hungry every day.[68] Holding back food aid or imposing economic sanctions will only worsen the hunger situation, with little real impact on the Taliban's behavior.

Leaving Afghanistan as the international community has will have long-term impacts. According to Index Mundi, the latest demographic data from Afghanistan shows that 63.5 percent of the population is younger than 24 years. There are 7.6 million Afghan children between the ages of 10 and 19.[69] Today, the average age of the Afghan population is 18.6 years.[70] This represents an incredible pool of recruits for extremist groups, including the Taliban, to train and equip these young minds not with knowledge but rather with radical ideologies. Recent history has made clear what happens when unemployed, dissatisfied, and uneducated young people fall victim to the Islamic State and the Taliban's propaganda machines. Afghanistan will become a breeding ground for extremists poised to be used by forces like China, Russia, and others against the world to achieve their goals in the region and beyond.

[68] "Afghanistan: WFP Committed to Averting Humanitarian Crisis as One in Three People Go Hungry," World Food Programme, 17 August 2021.

[69] "Afghanistan Demographic Profile," Index Mundi, accessed 31 May 2021.

[70] Richard Giasy, "The Afghan People: Observing Nearly 40 Years of Violent Conflict," *Write Peace* (blog), SIPRI, 5 October 2017.

CONCLUSION

In March 2005, more than 100 countries and international agencies came together in Paris, France, to discuss the effectiveness of international aid. The overall aim was to improve the quality of aid and its impact on development in other countries. International development experts presented their professional proposals on what works and does not work with aid. As a result, the *Paris Declaration on Aid Effectiveness* was created, based on development efforts grounded in the firsthand experience of these field workers and professionals.[1]

The *Paris Declaration on Aid Effectiveness* is a practical, action-oriented guide to help improve the quality of aid and its impact on development. It provides a series of specific implementation guidelines and establishes a system to ensure that donors and aid recipients hold each other accountable for their commitments. It is formulated around the following five central pillars.[2]

1. **Ownership**: donor recipient countries must set their own strategies for poverty reduction, improve their institutions, and tackle corruption. Recipient countries ought to own the strategic development of plans for themselves

---

[1] *Paris Declaration on Aid Effectiveness* (Paris, France: Organisation for Economic Co-operation and Development Publishing, 2005), http://dx.doi.org/10.1787/9789264098084-en.

[2] *Paris Declaration on Aid Effectiveness*, 9–10.

since they have a better understanding of local issues, obstacles, opportunities, and prospects.

2. **Alignment**: donor countries must align with strategic objectives developed by the recipient countries and use local systems to further the cause of poverty reduction.

3. **Harmonization**: donor countries must coordinate, simplify procedures, and share information to avoid duplication. The host country is best served when multiple donors coordinate their development efforts to eliminate inefficiencies.

4. **Results**: host countries and donors must place an emphasis on measuring their development results.

5. **Mutual accountability**: both donor and recipient countries are accountable for the results.

The question remains as to whether the government of Afghanistan and the international community practiced these guidelines for effective delivery of aid during the past 20 years.

At the Kabul conference in 2010, the government of Afghanistan presented a development strategy that included National Priority Programs (NPP). They also committed to undertake significant reform measures in the rule of law, elections, and human rights. In return, donors agreed to channel at least 50 percent of their aid through the Afghan national budget. They also agreed to align 80 percent of their spending with NPP.[3]

At the Tokyo conference in 2012, the *Tokyo Mutual Accountability Framework* (TMAF) was established in coordination with donors and the government of Afghanistan. It offered a set of commitments made by both the government and donors to act as counterbalancing influences by all parties involved in development.[4]

The London conference in 2014 was a reaffirmation of the Tokyo commitments under the TMAF. Once again, the same set of commitments were made by the donors and the Afghan government. Donors agreed to align their priorities with the government's NPP, and the government promised to deliver on a set of deliverables outlined in the TMAF by the end of 2015.[5]

Finally, at the Brussels conference in 2016, the government of Afghanistan presented the *Afghan National Peace and Development Framework* (ANPDF) and agreed to a set of 24 deliverables under the new *Self-Reliance through Mutual Accountability Framework* (SMAF). While the acronyms of these deliverables and strategic documents changed over time, the reality on

---

[3] "Kabul Conference Communique" (paper presented at the International Conference on Afghanistan, Kabul, 20 July 2010).

[4] "Tokyo Mutual Accountability Framework," USAID, 8 July 2012.

[5] "Afghanistan and International Community: Commitments to Reforms and Renewed Partnership" (paper from the London Conference on Afghanistan, 4 December 2014).

the ground for the poor and needy improved very little.[6]

Given that each conference on Afghanistan in the last decade led to billions of dollars in aid to the country, it is imperative to assess the effectiveness of the aid based on the factors provided by the *Paris Declaration on Aid Effectiveness*.

Ownership

The government of Afghanistan had developed at least two large strategic documents in the last 10 years: the *Afghanistan National Development Strategy* (ANDS) and the ANPDF. In conjunction, the government had set various NPP through a consultative cabinet process. The NPP were then funded through the national budget process, and the line ministries were tasked with implementing the programs.[7] The government of Afghanistan had developed a rudimentary process to claim full ownership of the development agenda in theory.

In return, donors made commitments in all the previous conferences that they would provide at least 50 percent of development aid through the government national budget and align 80 percent of their spend-

---

[6] *Afghanistan National Development Strategy: First Annual Report (2008/09)* (Washington, DC: International Monetary Fund, 2009); *Afghanistan National Peace and Development Framework (ANPDF) 2017 to 2021* (Kabul: Ministry of Finance, Islamic Republic of Afghanistan, 2016); *Self-Reliance through Mutual Accountability Framework (SMAF)* (Kabul: Islamic Republic of Afghanistan, 2015); and *National Infrastructure Plan, 2017–2021* (Kabul: Ministry of Finance, Islamic Republic of Afghanistan, 2016).

[7] Katerina Oskarsson, *Second International Tokyo Conference on Afghanistan* (Brussels, Belgium: Civil-Military Fusion Centre, North Atlantic Treaty Organization, 2012).

ing with the NPP. However, according to the Afghan government, during 2012–14 only $4.4 billion, or 25 percent of total development aid, had been channeled through the national budget.[8] While the government of Afghanistan had made good on its promise in terms of building a national strategy, donors had failed to meet their commitment to spending through the national budget. Key funding decisions for the NPP were not made in Kabul at the Ministry of Finance or by the president's office, but in the capitals of donor countries. This contrasts sharply with how the Marshall Plan process was conducted, in which the recipient countries were asked to develop the programs that were then funded by the plan.

Alignment

The second aid effectiveness pillar of the *Paris Declaration on Aid Effectiveness* calls for the alignment of donor aid with the NPP developed by the government of Afghanistan. On the surface, this should be an easy task. However, donors pick and choose parts of the NPP that were appealing to their constituents at home or to their public image around the world. For instance, the agricultural sector NPP requires massive investment for irrigation, infrastructure, market access, training, etc. A large number of donors will agree to fund the most attractive and visible portion of the program, such as the market access component. While this component receives massive amounts of aid, the irrigation, infra-

---

[8] *Citizens Budget* (Kabul: Ministry of Finance, Islamic Republic of Afghanistan, 2021).

structure, and training aspects are largely underfunded or not funded at all. Market access without agricultural products or road systems means absolutely nothing to the farmer in particular and to the development of the sector at large.[9]

Harmonization

Harmonization calls for a coordinated approach to program development by donors. It asks for information sharing across the board with all stakeholders involved to avoid duplication and reduce inefficiencies. According to the Afghan government, donor fragmentation has been widespread in Afghanistan. With competing interests, donors largely bypass government systems to avoid accountability. However, several platforms including the Afghan Reconstruction Trust Fund (ARTF) have created a harmonized process for 33 donors to coordinate their activities in the country. The ARTF has remained a vital tool for pooled funding with low transaction costs, enhanced transparency, and increased accountability.[10] It also provides a platform for policy debate and a consensus-building opportunity for donors and the government of Afghanistan.

Results and Mutual Accountability

The ultimate goal is to achieve good results from a development program. The *Paris Declaration on Aid Effectiveness* calls for results that are measurable to hold the

[9] *Paris Declaration on Aid Effectiveness.*

[10] "Afghanistan Reconstruction Trust Fund (ARTF)—Donor Contributions—BETA," World Bank Group Finances, accessed 21 July 2021.

parties accountable. In Afghanistan, plenty of reports, assessments, and evaluations of development programs are presented widely. However, none of them hold anyone accountable for the shortfalls or lack of development that existed. This lack of accountability has added significantly to corruption in the government and among development practitioners.[11]

The focus of development in Afghanistan has been primarily on the ability to deliver output rather than outcome. By focusing on output, donors and the government can easily show progress with little regard to the overall impact of their aid intervention on the development of Afghanistan. Ribbon-cutting ceremonies for newly built roads and bridges are widely attended by government officials and donor country representatives. However, when the road starts to erode or the bridge begins to crumble within a year, no one is held accountable for the poor quality of materials used.

An Aid-Dependent Economy

According to the World Bank, Afghanistan's GDP has increased on average annually by more than 6.6 percent during the last 17 years. The largest percentage increase was in 2009, with more than 21 percent GDP growth; the lowest was in 2011, with only 0.43 percent.[12] When GDP figures are compared with U.S. assistance numbers, the trend data parallels the other.

Development aid has created a heavily dependent Afghan economy, which is difficult to sustain as donor

---

[11] *Paris Declaration on Aid Effectiveness*, 8.
[12] "Afghanistan: Overview," World Bank, accessed 31 May 2021.

Figure 41. U.S. aid compared with Afghanistan's GDP growth, 2009–20, USD billions

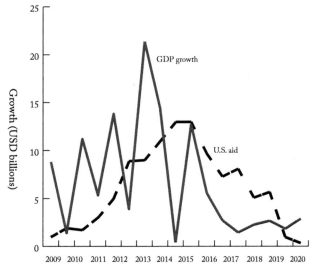

Sources: "Afghanistan: Overview," World Bank; and "Foreign Aid Explorer," USAID, 2021.

assistance continues to decrease or dry up altogether as a result of donor fatigue (figure 41).[13]

Most Afghans are concerned about the Taliban's return to power in the government. They fear the nominal gains of the last 20 years, including girls returning to

---

[13] Figure 41 shows the Afghan GDP growth and the U.S. aid trends from 2003 to 2019. Note that a large amount of U.S. assistance during 2010 and 2011 spurred massive economic growth. In 2018 and 2019, as foreign aid to Afghanistan decreased, economic growth contracted as well.

Figure 42. Twitter response to AUAF closure Source: Barnett R. Rubin, courtesy of Twitter.

school, women's rights, human rights, and freedom of speech, will be lost.[14] However, the Taliban may not be as big of a threat to the gains of the last two decades as aid dependence, which is a major risk to the future of Afghanistan.

For example, in late 2019, the news broke that the American University of Afghanistan (AUAF) would close due to a lack of funding by USAID.[15] The U.S. government had been the main source of funding for this university since its inception in 2006. Dr. Barnett R. Rubin, a well-known American political scientist and a leading expert on Afghanistan, tweeted in response to the closure of AUAF (figure 42).

---

[14] Ayesha Tanzeem, "Afghans Fear Taliban Return to Power after Withdrawal of US Forces," *VOA News*, 4 May 2021.

[15] Rod Nordland, "U.S.-Funded Afghan College Is under Scrutiny for Missing Millions, Officials Say," *New York Times*, 30 May 2019.

The total cost of the Marshall Plan was $17 billion over four years. When adjusted for inflation, the purchasing power of $17 billion in 1949 is equivalent to $138.8 billion in 2019. This historic amount of aid by the United States was distributed across 16 different countries in Europe, including the United Kingdom, France, and Germany. The Marshall Plan helped jump-start the European economy, which resulted in a prosperous continent. Economic output increased by 60 percent in four years. The postwar economic development in Europe represents the most astonishing feat in modern history. While it may be difficult to draw a direct connection between American aid and the economic growth that followed, for the most part, the Marshall Plan played the role of a stimulus that triggered a chain of events leading to massive economic growth in the years that followed.[16]

In Afghanistan, however, the United States has spent (by some estimates) more than $1 trillion and suffered more than 2,000 U.S. troops killed and at least 20,000 injured during the last 20 years. This massive American investment in nation-building efforts in Afghanistan has generated few significant achievements and Afghanistan is no safer than it was 20 years ago.[17] The Afghan economy is no better off than it was under Taliban rule in the 1990s. And as the United States has withdrawn its military presence, the faith of the country

---

[16] John Agnew and J. Nicholas Entrikin, eds., *The Marshall Plan Today: Model and Metaphor* (New York: Routledge, 2004), 14.

[17] Frank Gardner, "20 Years in Afghanistan: Was It Worth It?," BBC News, 17 April 2021.

lies at the hands of warlords, the "political elite," and, worse yet, the Taliban.[18]

Recommendations: Helping Afghanistan Help Itself

Afghanistan needs an economic recovery program and not a humanitarian relief effort. The current ad hoc and humanitarian relief-oriented assistance has made little impact on the economy of Afghanistan. A different, coherent approach is defined as increased agricultural and industrial production, restoration of sound budgeting and finances, and stimulation of international trade among neighboring countries and beyond.

First, a massive intervention like the Marshall Plan with a definite timeframe is required to ignite the Afghan economy. Rather than having a donor conference on Afghanistan every four years, where limited funds are raised for development purposes, the international community must commit to a larger amount of one-time aid to Afghanistan. How the resources are gathered, pooled, and spent is just as critical. As with the Marshall Plan, the United States was the single source of aid money, and it channeled all grants through an independent funding and monitoring mechanism: the Economic Cooperation Administration (ECA). The World Bank or any other multilateral organization could serve as a similar independent body to channel the funds for Afghanistan.

Second, funds must be invested heavily in areas directly or indirectly associated with the private sector. This

---

[18] Sarah Almukhtar and Rod Nordland, "What Did the U.S. Get for $2 Trillion in Afghanistan?," *New York Times*, 10 December 2019.

market-oriented development approach should include individual entrepreneurs or businesses at its heart and not the government. Businesses could be loaned money for a start-up or expansion, which could be repaid with little to no interest. The amount could then be loaned to other businesses. This more transparent cycle means that all money spent on public projects would come from loans, most of which would then be repaid to the fund. It also helps ensure a focus on restoring commercial infrastructure, such as roads, bridges, supply chains, banks, telecommunications networks, and other institutions, which would further boost economic activity.

Third, the government of Afghanistan, Talib or non-Talib, must make economic policy reforms to support its domestic private sector. These will make it easier for all businesses, from start-up entrepreneurs to midsize manufacturing and larger enterprises, to thrive. The budget process must be reformed. It must be made more market-oriented, efficient, and transparent. Confidence in the financial market must be restored so the public can use banks to save their money, which in turn can be loaned out to businesses. All trade barriers must also be removed, thereby increasing the markets and prospects for the entire region through increased trade.

Finally, and most crucially, it must be ensured that each technical and financial assistance component contributes as directly as possible to the long-term objectives.

Future Research

According to former finance minister Eklil A. Hakimi, the "ultimate goal of the Afghan government must be to achieve zero aid."[19] In other words, he would like to see Afghanistan become a self-sufficient nation capable of providing for itself without relying on foreign aid. It is necessary to investigate how this could be accomplished. Perhaps the next research project will concentrate on learning from South Korea's experience of transitioning from desperation to prosperity, from aid recipient to aid donor country.[20]

In addition, at the recent 2021 G7 meeting, U.S. president Joseph R. Biden Jr. proposed that Western nations develop a plan to compete with China's Belt and Road Initiative. The Build Back Better World initiative intends to address the enormous infrastructure needs of low and middle-income countries. The idea is to help narrow the $40 trillion infrastructure needed in poor nations that has been made worse by the COVID-19 pandemic.[21] Conversely, the Chinese government's Belt and Road Initiative is feeding immense investments through various channels to fund massive infrastructure projects along the Silk Road. Because Afghanistan is strategically located along the Silk Road, it is critical to study how any government in Kabul can capitalize on the global rivalry between East and West to develop its infrastructure in tandem with its economy.

---

[19] Eklil A. Hakimi, phone conversation with author, 2021.
[20] Kongdan Oh, "Korea's Path from Poverty to Philanthropy," Brookings, 14 June 2010.
[21] "President Biden and G7 Leaders Launch Build Back Better World (B3W) Partnership," press release, White House, 12 June 2021.

SELECTED BIBLIOGRAPHY

"1400 National Budget Document." Ministry of Finance, Islamic Republic of Afghanistan, 9 March 2021.

Adili, Ali Yawar. *The Results of Afghanistan's 2018 Parliamentary Elections: A New, but Incomplete Wolesi Jirga*. Kabul: Afghanistan Analysts Network, 2020.

Afghan Const. § 3, art. LXI.

Afghan National Army: DOD May Have Spent up to $28 Million More than Needed to Procure Camouflage Uniforms that May Be Inappropriate for the Afghan Environment, SIGAR-17-48-SP. Arlington, VA: Special Inspector General for Afghanistan Reconstruction, 2017.

"Afghan President Says He Left Country to Avoid Bloodshed." *Reuters*, 15 August 2021.

"Afghan Remittances from Iran Total $500 Million Annually, Says UN Report." UN News, 7 December 2008.

"Afghan Vote Results: Karzai at 54.6 Percent." NBC News, 16 September 2009.

"Afghan War Casualty Report: June 2021." *New York Times*, 4 August 2021.

"Afghanistan (AFG): Exports, Imports, and Trade Partners." Observatory of Economic Complexity, 2019.

"Afghanistan Aid: Donors Promise $15.2bn in Brussels." BBC News, 5 October 2016.

"Afghanistan among 'Deadliest Countries' for Reporters: RSF." *TOLO News*, 21 April 2020.

"Afghanistan and International Community: Commitments to Reforms and Renewed Partnership." Paper presented at the London Conference on Afghanistan, 4 December 2014.

Afghanistan Annual Report, 2017. New York: UNICEF, 2017.

"Afghanistan: Civilian Casualties Exceed 10,000 for Sixth Straight Year." UN News, 22 February 2020.

"Afghanistan Demographics Profile." Index Mundi, accessed 31 May 2021.

"Afghanistan: Electoral Complaints Commission." Press release, United Nations Office for the Coordination of Humanitarian Affairs, 12 May 2009.

Afghanistan Human Development Report, 2020: Pitfalls and Promise. Kabul: UNDP Afghanistan Country Office, 2020.

Afghanistan: Improving the Development Effectiveness of the Afghanistan Infrastructure Trust Fund. Manila, Philippines: Asian Development Bank, 2020.

Afghanistan in 2004: A Survey of the Afghan People. Kabul, Afghanistan: Asia Foundation, 2004.

Afghanistan in 2008: A Survey of the Afghan People. Kabul, Afghanistan: Asia Foundation, 2008.

"Afghanistan—Journey to Self-Reliance: FY 2021 Country Roadmap." USAID, accessed 8 July 2021.

Afghanistan Living Conditions Study, 2016–17. Kabul: Central Statistics Organization (CSO) of the Government of the Islamic Republic of Afghanistan and ICON International, 2016.

Afghanistan National Development Strategy, 1387–1391 (2008–2013): A Strategy for Security, Governance, Economic Growth & Poverty Reduction. Kabul: Islamic Republic of Afghanistan, 2010.

Afghanistan National Development Strategy: An Interim Strategy for Security, Governance, Economic Growth & Poverty Reduction, vol. 1. Kabul: Islamic Republic of Afghanistan, 2005.

Afghanistan National Development Strategy: First Annual Report (2008/09). Washington, DC: International Monetary Fund, 2009.

Afghanistan National Peace and Development Framework (ANPDF) 2017 to 2021. Kabul: Ministry of Finance, Islamic Republic of Afghanistan, 2016.

"Afghanistan: Overview." World Bank, accessed 31 May 2021.

"Afghanistan Products Exports, Imports, Tariffs by Country and Region, 2018." WITS Data, World Bank, accessed 19 July 2021.

Afghanistan Reconstruction: Progress Made in Constructing Roads, but Assessments for Determining Impact and a Sustainable Maintenance Program Are Needed, Report No. GAO-08-689. Washington, DC: Government Accountability Office, 2008.

"Afghanistan Reconstruction Trust Fund (ARTF)—Donor Contributions—BETA." World Bank Group Finances, accessed 21 July 2021.

"Afghanistan." Reuters COVID-19 Tracker, accessed 10 September 2021.

Afghanistan Security: Efforts to Establish Army and Police Have Made Progress, but Future Plans Need to Be Better Defined, GAO-05-575. Washington, DC: Government Accountability Office, 2005.

Afghanistan Study Group Final Report, February 2021. Washington, DC: U.S. Institute of Peace, 2021.

"Afghanistan: Taliban Refuses to Hand over Bin Laden." Radio Free Europe, 21 September 2001.

"Afghanistan." Transparency.org, accessed 28 January 2021.

Afghanistan: U.S.- and Internationally-Funded Roads (GAO-09-626SP), an E-supplement to GAO-09-473SP. Washington, DC: Government Accountability Office, 2009.

Afghanistan: Voluntary Repatriation, Response Snapshot. Geneva, Switzerland: UN High Commissioner for Refugees, 2019.

"Afghanistan: WFP Committed to Averting Humanitarian Crisis as One in Three People Go Hungry." World Food Programme, 17 August 2021.

Afghanistan's Economy to Rebound in 2021 Despite Challenges. Manila, Philippines: Asian Development Bank, 2021.

"Afghanistan's Ghani Says 45,000 Security Personnel Killed since 2014." BBC News, 25 January 2019.

Agnew, John, and J. Nicholas Entrikin, eds. *The Marshall Plan Today: Model and Metaphor*. New York: Routledge, 2004.

"A Historical Timeline of Afghanistan." PBS News Hour, 31 December 2014.

Ajayi, Kunle. *International Administration and Economic Relations in Changing World*. Ilorin, Nigeria: Majab Publishers, 2002.

Almukhtar, Sarah, and Rod Nordland. "What Did the U.S. Get for $2 Trillion in Afghanistan?." *New York Times*, 10 December 2019.

Amiri, Mohammad Abid. "Road Reconstruction in Post-Conflict Afghanistan: A Cure or a Curse?." *International Affairs Review* 11, no. 2 (2013).

ANA Proprietary Camouflaged Uniforms, SIGAR-17-48-SP. Arlington, VA: Special Inspector General for Afghanistan Reconstruction (SIGAR), 2017.

April–June 2019 Quarterly Report to the People of Afghanistan. Kabul: Independent Joint Anti-Corruption Monitoring and Evaluation Committee, 2019.

Archer, Kristjan. "Inside Afghanistan: Job Market Outlook Bleakest on Record." Gallup World Poll, 9 September 2019.

Associated Press. "Finger-thin Undersea Cables Tie World Together." NBC News, 31 January 2008.

Baldor, Lolita C., and Kathy Gannon. "Military Blindsided by Trump's New Afghan Troop Withdrawal." AP News, 8 October 2020.

Berg, Kim. "Demonstrating for Change." Deutschland, accessed 15 July 2019.

Behrman, Greg. *The Most Noble Adventure: The Marshall Plan and the Time When America Helped Save Europe.* New York: Free Press, 2007.

Biden, Joseph R. "Remarks by President Biden on Afghanistan." Speech, East Room, White House, 16 August 2021.

———. "Remarks by President Biden on the Drawdown of U.S. Forces in Afghanistan." Speech, East Room, White House, 8 July 2021.

———. "Remarks by President Biden on the Way Forward in Afghanistan." Speech, Treaty Room, White House, 14 April 2021.

Bikus, Zach. "Inside Afghanistan: Stability in Institutions Remains Elusive." Gallup World Report, 4 September 2019.

Boone, Jon. "Afghanistan Election Challenger Abdullah Abdullah Pulls Out of Runoff." *Guardian*, 1 November 2009.

Boudreau, Frank G. "Nutrition in War and Peace." *Milbank Quarterly* 83, no. 4 (2005). https://doi.org/10.1111/j.1468-0009.2005.00394.x.

Brown Jr., William Adams, and Redvers Opie. *American Foreign Assistance.* Washington, DC: Brookings Institution, 1953.

"Brussels Conference on Afghanistan: October 4–5, 2016." Bureau of South and Central Asian Affairs, Department of State, 12 December 2016.

"Brussels Conference on Afghanistan: Realizing Afghanistan's Economic Potential and Reinforcing the Role of Women." Press release, European Commission, 4 October 2016.

Building on Success: The London Conference on Afghanistan—The Afghanistan Compact. Brussels, Belgium: North Atlantic Treaty Organization, 2006.

"Bush Announces Strikes against Taliban." *Washington Post*, 7 October 2001.

Bush, George W. *Decision Points.* New York: Random House, 2010.

———. "President Bush Discusses Progress in Afghanistan, Global War on Terror." Speech, Mayflower Hotel, Washington, DC, 15 February 2007.

———. "President Outlines War Effort." Speech, Virginia Military Institute, Lexington, VA, 17 April 2002.

———. "Presidential Return." C-SPAN, 14 October 2001, 3:18 min.

"Bush Rejects Taliban Offer to Hand Bin Laden Over." *Guardian*, 14 October 2001.

Cancho, Cesar A., and Tejesh Pradhan. "Mitigating the Poverty Implications of COVID-19 in Afghanistan." *End Poverty in South Asia* (blog), World Bank, 16 August 2020.

Carlsson, Jerker, Gloria Somolekae, and Nicolas van de Walle, eds. *Foreign Aid in Africa: Learning from Country Experience.* Uppsala, Sweden: Nordic Africa Institute, 1997.

"Casualty Status." Press release, Department of Defense, 19 July 2021.

"Celebrations, Confusion as Kandahar Falls." CNN, 7 December 2001.

Chivers, C. J. "Trouble on a Vital Road in Afghanistan." *New York Times*, 3 December 2007.

"Cholecystectomy (Gallbladder Removal)." Department of Surgery, University of California-San Francisco, accessed 16 July 2021.

Citizens Budget. Kabul: Ministry of Finance, Islamic Republic of Afghanistan, 2021.

"Co-chairs' Summary of Conclusions: The International Conference on Reconstruction Assistance to Afghanistan." Paper presented at International Conference on Reconstruction Assistance to Afghanistan, Tokyo, Japan, 21–22 January 2002.

"Commission Releases Disputed 2014 Afghan Election Results." *Reuters*, 24 February 2016.

"Communique on the Brussels Conference on Afghanistan." Press release, Department of State, 5 October 2016.

Comprehensive Needs Assessment for Reconstruction in the Transport Sector—Afghanistan. Mandaluyong, Philippines: Asian Development Bank, 2002.

Crawford, Neta C., and Catherine Lutz. *Human Cost of Post-9/11 Wars: Direct War Deaths in Major War Zones, Afghanistan and Pakistan (October 2001–October 2019); Iraq (March*

2003–October 2019); Syria (September 2014–October 2019); Yemen (October 2002–October 2019); and Other. Providence, RI: Watson Institute for International and Public Affairs, Brown University, 2019.

Dale, Catherine. *Operation Iraqi Freedom: Strategies, Approaches, Results, and Issues for Congress.* Washington, DC: Congressional Research Service, 2008.

Daley, Suzanne. "After the Attacks: The Alliance; For First Time, NATO Invokes Joint Defense Pact with U.S." *New York Times,* 13 September 2001.

Dao, James. "A Nation Challenged: The President; Bush Sets Role for U.S. in Afghan Rebuilding." *New York Times,* 18 April 2002.

"Declaration of the International Conference in Support of Afghanistan." Press release, United Nations, 12 June 2008.

De Long, J. Bradford, and Barry Eichengreen. "The Marshall Plan: History's Most Successful Structural Adjustment Program." Paper presented at the Centre for Economic Performance and Landeszentralbank Hamburg Conference on Post–World War II European Reconstruction, Hamburg, Germany, 57 September 1991.

Derksen, Deedee. *The Politics of Disarmament and Rearmament in Afghanistan.* Washington, DC: U.S. Institute of Peace, 2015.

Diamond, Jeremy. "Donald Trump: Afghanistan War a 'Mistake,' but Troops Need to Stay." CNN, 6 October 2015.

Divided Responsibility: Lessons from U.S. Security Sector Assistance Efforts in Afghanistan. Arlington, VA: SIGAR, 2019.

"Donors' Aid Pledges for Afghanistan." *Reuters,* 12 June 2008.

EASO Country of Origin Information Report: Afghanistan Recruitment by Armed Groups. Luxembourg: Publications Office of the European Union, 2016.

"Education: Providing Quality Education for All." UNICEF, 2018.

"Education System Profiles: Education in Afghanistan." World Education News & Reviews, 6 September 2016.

Enhancing Connectivity and Freight in Central Asia: Case-Specific Policy Analysis, International Transport Forum Policy Papers No. 71. Paris, France: OECD Publishing, 2019.

"Every Man in Mosul Ordered to Grow a Beard." Radio Free Europe, 29 April 2015.

Exploring Three Strategies for Afghanistan: Hearing before the

Committee on Foreign Relations, 111th Cong., 1st Sess., 16 September 2009.

Farhad, Mohammed Nader. "Manage Afghan Labour Migration to Curb Irregular Flow to Iran, Study Urges." United Nations High Commissioner for Refugees, 11 December 2008.

Ferguson, Niall. "Dollar Diplomacy: How Much Did the Marshall Plan Really Matter?." *New Yorker*, 20 August 2007.

Ferrarello, Molli. "What 'America First' Means for US Foreign Aid." *Brookings Now* (blog), Brookings, 27 July 2017.

Fields, Mark, and Ramsha Ahmed. *A Review of the 2001 Bonn Conference and Application to the Road Ahead in Afghanistan.* Washington, DC: Institute for National Strategic Studies, National Defense University, 2011.

Fighting Corruption in Afghanistan: A Roadmap for Strategy and Action. N.p.: Asian Development Bank, UK Department for International Development, United Nations Development Programme, United Nations Office on Drugs and Crime, and the World Bank, 2007.

Finnegan, Conor. "US Signs Historic Deal with Taliban, Trump Announces, Beginning End of US War in Afghanistan and Withdrawal of American Troops." ABC News, 29 February 2020.

Fisher, Max. "In White House, Biden Pushes Back on Afghanistan." *Atlantic*, 14 October 2009.

"Foreign Aid Explorer." USAID, accessed 17 August 2021.

Framer, Ben. "Kabul-Kandahar Highway Is a Symbol of What's Gone Wrong in Afghanistan." *Telegraph*, 9 September 2012.

Frankel, Jeffrey A., and David Romer. *Trade and Growth: An Empirical Investigation*, NBER Working Paper No. 5476. Cambridge, MA: National Bureau of Economic Research, 1996, https://doi.org/10.3386/w5476.

Gall, Carlotta. "Afghanistan's Kabul-Kandahar Highway: A Lifeline Plagued with Insurgents." *New York Times*, 13 August 2008.

Gannon, Kathy. "Afghan Refugees Tell UN: 'We Need Peace, Land to Go Home'." ABC News, 17 February 2020.

———. "After 17 Years, Many Afghans Blame US for Unending War." AP News, 13 November 2018.

———. "Taliban Cheer Trump Tweet Promising Early Troop Withdrawal." ABC News, 8 October 2020.

Gardner, Frank. "20 Years in Afghanistan: Was It Worth It?." BBC News, 17 April 2021.

"GDP per Capita, Constant PPP Dollars, v. 27." Gapminder, 2017.

"Gender Development Index (GDI)." Human Development Reports, United Nations Development Programme, accessed 22 May 2021.

George, Susannah, Claire Parker, John Hudson, Karen DeYoung, Dan Lamothe, and Bryan Pietsch. "Afghan Government Collapses as Taliban Sweeps in, U.S. Sends More Troops to Aid Chaotic Withdrawal." *Washington Post*, 15 August 2021.

Ghani, Ahmadzai. *Manifesto of Change and Continuity Team*. Kabul: Islamic Republic of Afghanistan, 2014.

"Ghani Takes the Oath of Afghan President. His Rival Does, Too." *New York Times*, 9 March 2020.

Ghazi, Zabihullah, and Fahim Abed. "Demand for Pakistan Visas Sets Off Deadly Stampede in Afghanistan." *New York Times*, 27 October 2020.

Giasy, Richard. "The Afghan People: Observing Nearly 40 Years of Violent Conflict." *Write Peace* (blog), Stockholm International Peace Research Institute, 5 October 2017.

Glinski, Stephanie. "Food Prices Soar under Coronavirus Threat in Afghanistan." *New Humanitarian*, 7 April 2020.

———. " 'No Profit, No Food': Lockdown in Kabul Prompts Hunger Fears." *Guardian*, 1 April 2020.

Global Law and Order, 2020. Washington, DC: Gallup, 2020.

"Global Trends: Forced Displacement in 2018." UNHCR, 20 June 2019.

Good, Chris. "When and Why Did Americans Turn against the War in Afghanistan?." *Atlantic*, 22 June 2011.

Graham-Harrison, Emma. "Afghan Forces Suffering Too Many Casualties, Says Top NATO Commander." *Guardian*, 2 September 2013.

Graham-Harrison, Emma, and Akhtar Mohammad Makoii. " 'The Taliban Took Years of My Life': The Afghan Women Living in the Shadow of War." *Guardian*, 9 February 2019.

Gray, Andrew. "Obama Orders 17,000 U.S. Troops to Afghanistan." *Reuters*, 17 February 2009.

Gukumure, S. "Interrogating Foreign Aid and Sustainable Development Conundrum in African Countries; A Zimbabwe

Experience of Debt Trap and Service Delivery." *International Journal of Politics and Good Governance* 3, no. 3.4 (4th quarter, 2012).

Gul, Ayaz. "Afghan Civilian Casualties Spiked 29%, UN Reports." *VOA News*, 14 April 2021.

———. "Afghan Official: 600 Freed Taliban Prisoners Rearrested." *VOA News*, 24 January 2021.

———. "Pompeo Defends Trump's Afghan Peace Plan, Ensuing 'Incredible Progress'." *VOA News*, 2 January 2021.

———. "Survey: Afghans Pay $3 Billion in Bribes Annually." *VOA News*, 8 December 2018.

Hadid, Diaa. "U.S. Unconditional Withdrawal Rattles Afghanistan's Shaky Peace Talks." NPR, 29 April 2021.

Hammes, T. X. "Raising and Mentoring Security Forces in Afghanistan and Iraq." In Richard D. Hooker Jr. and Joseph J. Collins, eds., *Lessons Learned: Learning from the Long War*. Washington, DC: National Defense University Press, 2015.

Harrison, Mark, ed. *The Economics of World War II: Six Great Powers in International Comparison*. Cambridge, UK: Cambridge University Press, 1998, 1–42. https://doi.org/10.1017/CBO 9780511523632.

Harsch, Michael F., and Taylor Whitsell. "Afghans Don't Need U.S. Troops. They Need Islands of Stability." *Foreign Policy*, 20 April 2021.

Hein, David. "Lessons from the Marshall Plan: Liberty and Faith, Not Money and Power." *Hill*, 26 April 2018.

Heneghan, Tom. "Afghans Get Down to Details in UN Talks." *Reuters*, 28 November 2001.

Hicks, Tyler. "Intimidation and Fraud Observed in Afghan Election." *New York Times*, 23 August 2009.

"High-stakes Talks between Afghan Gov't, Taliban as Fighting Rages." *Al Jazeera*, 17 July 2021.

"History of the Marshall Plan." George C. Marshall Foundation, accessed 15 June 2021.

Hogan, Michael J. *The Marshall Plan: America, Britain, and the Reconstruction of Western Europe, 1947–1952*. Cambridge, UK: Cambridge University Press, 1987. https://doiorg/10 .1017/CBO9780511583728.

Human Development Reports. New York: United Nations Development Programme, 2021.

Ingram, George. "Myths about U.S. Foreign Aid." *Unpacked* (blog), Brookings, 7 April 2017.

Inspection and Evaluation Service. "Evaluation of UNHCR's Repatriation Operation to Mozambique." UNHCR, 1 February 1996.

Interagency Assessment of Afghanistan Police Training and Readiness, Department of State Report No. ISP-IQO-07-07, Department of Defense Report No. IE-2007-001. Washington, DC: Inspectors General, U.S. Department of State and U.S. Department of Defense, 2006.

"Interview with Karim Khurram about His New Book." YouTube, 26 August 2019, 1:20:21 min.

Intra-European Payments Plan, 1948–49. Washington, DC: World Bank, 1950.

"Iran Exports to Afghanistan." *Trading Economics*, July 2021.

"ISAF's Mission in Afghanistan (2001–2014) (Archived)." North Atlantic Treaty Organization, 1 September 2015.

Islam, Mafizul. *Roads Socio-Economic Impact Assessment: Kabul–Kandahar Road*. Kabul: USAID Afghanistan, 2008.

"I Won't Be a Doctor, and One Day You'll Be Sick": Girls' Access to Education in Afghanistan. New York: Human Rights Watch, 2017.

Jahanmal, Zabihullah. "Afghans Paid $1.6 Billion in Bribes in 2018: Report." *TOLO News*, 29 June 2020.

"Japan to Host Conference on Afghanistan in Early July." Japan International Cooperation Agency, May/June 2012.

Johnson, Katanga, and Anthony Esposito. "Afghan All-girl Robotics Team Members, Journalists Land in Mexico." *Reuters*. 25 August 2021.

Johnson, Kay. "Cash-poor Afghanistan Will Delay Paying Civil Servants: Finance Ministry Official." *Reuters*, 27 September 2014.

Joshi, Kamal. "Afghanistan: Taliban Announces Ban on Music in Public Places, Claims 'Forbidden in Islam'." *Republic World*, 26 August 2021.

"Kabul Conference Communique." Paper presented at the International Conference on Afghanistan, Kabul, 20 July 2010.

Kaplan, Fred. "The War in Afghanistan Was Doomed from the Start." *Slate* (blog), 9 December 2019.

Kelemen, Michele. "Relationship between Karzai, U.S. Deteriorates." NPR, 8 April 2010.

"Kennedy-Lugar Youth Exchange & Study Program." World Learning, accessed 19 July 2021.

Kerry, John F. "Senator Kerry on Afghanistan War." C-SPAN, 21 October 2009, 22:18 min.

Kesternich, Iris, Bettina Siflinger, James P. Smith, and Joachim K. Winter. *The Effects of World War II on Economic and Health Outcomes across Europe*, Rand Working Paper Series WR-917. Santa Monica, CA: Rand, 2012. https://doi.org /10.2139/ssrn.1992007.

Khalilzad, Zalmay. "Dedication Ceremony for the Phase I Completion, Kabul-Kandahar Highway." Speech, Durrani, Afghanistan, 16 December 2003.

Kirby, Jen. "NATO Allies Are Preparing for a Future without America's 'Forever Wars'." *Vox*, 31 August 2021.

Knickmeyer, Ellen. "Costs of the Afghanistan War, in Lives and Dollars." *AP News*, 17 August 2021.

Kurtzleben, Danielle. "How the U.S. Troop Levels in Afghanistan Have Changed under Obama." NPR, 6 July 2016.

Landler, Mark. "Obama Signs Pact in Kabul, Turning Page in Afghan War." *New York Times*, 2 May 2012.

"Leaving Afghanistan, U.S. General's Ghostly Image Books Place in History." *Reuters*, 31 August 2021.

Lee, Carol E. "Frustrated Military Officials Want Biden to Make a Decision on Afghanistan." NBC News, 8 April 2021.

Lee, Matthew, and Eric Tucker. "Was Biden Handcuffed by Trump's Taliban Deal in Doha?." *AP News*, 19 August 2021.

Lemire, Jonathan, and Deb Reichmann. "Trump Calls Off Secret Meeting with Taliban, Afghan Leaders." *AP News*, 7 September 2019.

Lesko, Jamieson. "Afghan Suburbia: Luxury Construction Boom Grips Kabul Despite Uncertain Future." NBC News, 28 September 2013.

"Life Expectancy (from Birth) from 1875 to 2020." Statista, accessed 9 July 2021.

Logan, Lara. "Kabul under Siege while America's Longest War Rages On." *60 Minutes*, CBS News, 14 January 2018.

Lowe, Keith. *Savage Continent: Europe in the Aftermath of World War II*. New York: St. Martin's Press, 2012.

Lushenko, Paul, Lance Van Auken, and Garrett Stebbins. "ISIS-K: Deadly Nuisance or Strategic Threat?." *Small Wars & In-*

surgencies 30, no. 2 (2019): 265–78. https://doi.org/10.108 0/09592318.2018.1546293.

Lyn, Tan Ee. "Death in Childbirth: A Health Scourge for Afghanistan." *Reuters*, 29 April 2008.

Machado, Barry. "Conceptualizing the Marshall Plan." In *In Search of a Usable Past: The Marshall Plan and Postwar Reconstruction Today*. Lexington, VA: George C. Marshall Foundation, 2007.

Macias, Amanda. "U.S. Winds down Kabul Mission after Helping Evacuate 116,000 People in Just over 2 Weeks." CNBC, 30 August 2021.

Mack, Robert T. *Raising the World's Standard of Living: The Coordination and Effectiveness of Point Four, United Nations Technical Assistance, and Related Programs*. New York: Citadel Press, 1953.

Madhani, Aamer, and Matthew Lee. "Biden to Pull US Troops from Afghanistan, End 'Forever War'." *AP News*, 14 April 2021.

Maizland, Lindsay. "U.S.-Taliban Peace Deal: What to Know." Council on Foreign Relations, 2 March 2020.

Marantzidis, Nikos. "The Greek Civil War (1944–1949) and the International Communist System." *Journal of Cold War Studies* 15, no. 4 (2013): 25–54.

Marshall, George C. "Remarks by the Secretary of State at Harvard University on 5 June 1947." Speech, Harvard University, Cambridge, MA, 5 June 1947, George C. Marshall Foundation Library.

"Marshall Plan, 1948." Office of the Historian, Foreign Service Institute, Department of State, accessed 7 July 2021.

"Mass Deportation from Iran May Cause Crisis, Official Warns." *New Humanitarian*, 27 February 2008.

Master National Budget, 2019. Kabul: Ministry of Finance, Islamic Republic of Afghanistan, 2019.

McCarthy, Justin. "Inside Afghanistan: Record Numbers Struggle to Afford Basics." Gallup World Poll, 26 August 2019.

McMaster, H. R., and Bradley Bowman. "In Afghanistan, the Tragic Toll of Washington Delusion." *Wall Street Journal*, 15 August 2021.

"Median Age of the World Population from 1990 to 2015 and a Forecast until 2100, by Fertility Variant." Statista, accessed 19 July 2021.

Mengli, Ahmed, Mushtaq Yusufzai, Rhea Mogul, and Andrea Mitchell. "Afghan President Flees Country as U.S. Rushes to Exit with Taliban on Brink of Power." NBC News, 15 August 2021.

Milner, Helen V., and Dustin Tingley, ed. "Introduction to the Geopolitics of Foreign Aid." In *Geopolitics of Foreign Aid*, vol. 1. Cheltenham, UK: Edward Elgar, 2013.

Monitoring of Drug Flows in Afghanistan. Kabul, Afghanistan: United Nations Office on Drugs and Crime, 2007.

Morelli, Vincent, and Paul Belkin. *NATO in Afghanistan: A Test of the Transatlantic Alliance*. Washington, DC: Congressional Research Service, 2009.

Moyo, Dambisa. *Dead Aid: Why Aid Is Not Working and There Is a Way for Africa*. New York: Farrar, Straus, and Giroux, 2009.

Naimark, Norman M. "Stalin and Europe in the Postwar Period, 1945–53: Issues and Problems." *Journal of Modern European History* 2, no. 1 (2004).

National Corruption Survey, 2018: Afghans' Perceptions and Experiences of Corruption. Kabul: Integrity Watch Afghanistan, 2018.

National Infrastructure Plan, 2017–2021. Kabul: Ministry of Finance, Islamic Republic of Afghanistan, 2016.

"National Priority Programs." Office of the Deputy Minister for Policy, Ministry of Finance, Islamic Republic of Afghanistan, 2016.

"NATO and Afghanistan." North Atlantic Treaty Organization, 6 July 2021.

Nelson, Craig. "U.S. Officials Walk Out of Meeting at Presidential Palace in Kabul." *Wall Street Journal*, 26 March 2019.

Neumann, Brian, Lisa Mundey, and Jon Mikolashek. *The United States Army in Afghanistan: Operation Enduring Freedom, March 2002–April 2005*. Fort Lesley J. McNair, Washington, DC: U.S. Army Center of Military History, 2002.

Nordland, Rod. "The Death Toll for Afghan Forces Is Secret. Here's Why." *New York Times*, 21 September 2018.

———. "U.S.-Funded Afghan College Is under Scrutiny for Missing Millions, Officials Say." *New York Times*, 30 May 2019.

Nordland, Rod, and Mujib Mashal. "Afghan National Security Chief Is Sidelined in His Own War." *New York Times*, 30 March 2019.

"Northern Alliance." In Jan Palmowski, *A Dictionary of Contemporary World History*, 3d ed. Oxford, UK: Oxford University Press, 2008. https://doi.org/10.1093/acref/9780 199295678.001.0001.

"Number of Fatalities among Western Coalition Soldiers Involved in the Execution of Operation Enduring Freedom from 2001 to 2020." Statista, 2021.

Obama, Barack H. "Remarks by the President on a New Strategy for Afghanistan and Pakistan." Speech, Dwight D. Eisenhower Executive Office Building, Washington, DC, 27 March 2009.

———. "The New Way Forward—The President's Address." Speech, U.S. Military Academy at West Point, NY, 1 December 2009.

Oh, Kongdan. "Korea's Path from Poverty to Philanthropy." Brookings, 14 June 2010.

Oliphant, Roland. "Women Will Not Work at Ministerial Level in Taliban Government." *Telegraph*, 1 September 2021.

Omid, Mir Haidar Shah. "ADB Predicts Decline in Afghanistan's Economic Growth." *TOLO News*, 15 September 2020.

Oskarsson, Katerina. *Second International Tokyo Conference on Afghanistan*. Brussels, Belgium: Civil-Military Fusion Centre, North Atlantic Treaty Organization, 2012.

"Pakistan and Afghanistan." Institute for the Study of War, accessed 20 July 2021.

"Pakistan Outrage after 'Nato Attack Kills Soldiers'." BBC News, 26 November 2011.

Paris Declaration and Accra Agenda for Action. Paris, France: Organisation for Economic Co-operation and Development Publishing, 2011.

Paris Declaration on Aid Effectiveness. Paris, France: Organisation for Economic Co-operation and Development Publishing, 2005, 9–10. http://dx.doi.org/10.1787/978 9264098084-en.

Perry, Walter L., and David Kassing. *Toppling the Taliban: Air-Ground Operations in Afghanistan, October 2001–June 2002*. Santa Monica, CA: Rand, 2015. https://doi.org /10.7249/RR381.

Peter, Tom A. "Afghanistan Still World's Top Opium Supplier, Despite 10 Years of US-led War." *Christian Science Monitor*, 11 October 2011.

————. "Paved Roads a Positive Legacy of Afghan War. But Who Fixes Potholes?." *Christian Science Monitor*, 2 February 2015.

"Poverty Pushing Youth into Arms of Taliban?." *New Humanitarian*, 27 February 2008.

"President Biden and G7 Leaders Launch Build Back Better World (B3W) Partnership." Press release, White House, 12 June 2021.

"President Bush Speaks at VMI, Addresses Middle East Conflict." CNN Transcripts, 17 April 2002.

"Presidential Candidates Debate." C-SPAN, 3 October 2000, 1:36:36 min.

Price, Gareth, and Hameed Hakimi. *Reconnecting Afghanistan: Lessons from Cross-border Engagement*. London, UK: Royal Institute of International Affairs, Chatham House, 2019.

Price, Harry Baynard. *The Marshall Plan and Its Meaning*. New York: Cornell University Press, 1955.

Proposed Grant for an Afghanistan Rural Access Project, No. 69508-AF. Washington, DC: World Bank, 2012.

Protecting Refugees: A Field Guide for NGOS. New York: United Nations High Commissioner for Refugees, 1999.

Quarterly Report for the Period October through December 1993. Washington, DC: Afghan Construction and Logistics Unit, USAID, 1994.

Quarterly Report to the United States Congress, Jan 30, 2017. Arlington, VA: Special Inspector General for Afghanistan Reconstruction, 2017.

Quarterly Report to the United States Congress, Jul 30, 2018. Arlington, VA: Special Inspector General for Afghanistan Reconstruction, 2018.

Rahman, Abdul. "Energy Sector Afghanistan: Importance of Renewable Energy for Afghanistan—"Renewable Energy for Sustainable Development." Presentation, International Conference on Renewable Energy in Central Asia: Creating Economic Sustainability to Solve Socio-Economic Challenges, Dushanbe, Tajikistan, 10–11 November 2009.

Rashid, Ahmed. *Taliban: Militant Islam, Oil and Fundamentalism in Central Asia*. New Haven, CT: Yale University Press, 2010.

"Record-high Opium Production in Afghanistan Creates Multiple Challenges for Region and Beyond, UN Warns." *UN News*, 21 May 2018.

"Reforms in Review Part 5: Reforming the Civil Service Commission and Public Sector." Office of the Deputy Minister for Policy, Ministry of Finance, 2018.

Reinhart, R. J., and Julie Ray. "Inside Afghanistan: Law and Order Becomes a Casualty of War." Gallup World Report, 19 August 2019.

Risen, James. "Costly Afghanistan Road Project Is Marred by Unsavory Alliances." *New York Times*, 1 May 2011.

Roggio, Bill. "Mapping Taliban Control in Afghanistan." *Long War Journal*, accessed 10 September 2021.

Rowlatt, Justin. "How the US Military's Opium War in Afghanistan Was Lost." BBC News, 25 April 2019.

Safi, Mariam, and Bismellah Alizada. *Integrating Afghanistan into the Belt and Road Initiative: Review, Analysis and Prospects*. Bonn, Germany: Friedrich Ebert Stiftung, 2018.

Sands, Chris. "Afghan Truck Drivers Quiver from Lawlessness, not Taliban." *San Francisco (CA) Chronicle*, 28 May 2007.

Schelling, T. "American Foreign Assistance." *World Politics* 7, no. 4 (1955): 606–26. https://doi.org/10.2307/2009059.

Schnell, Mychael. "Taliban Acting Education Minister Says Mixed Gender University Classes Will Be Banned." *Hill*, 30 August 2021.

Schultz, Dante, "The Urgent Need to Expand Afghanistan's Electricity Supplies." Caspian Policy Center, 29 January 2021.

Schwarz, Jon, and Robert Mackey. "All the Times Donald Trump Said the U.S. Should Get Out of Afghanistan." *Intercept*, 21 August 2017.

Scobell, Andrew, Bonny Lin, Howard J. Shatz, Michael Johnson, Larry Hanauer, Michael S. Chase, Astrid Stuth Cevallos, Ivan W. Rasmussen, Arthur Chan, Aaron Strong, Eric Warner, and Logan Ma. *At the Dawn of Belt and Road: China in the Developing World*. Santa Monica, CA: Rand, 2018. https://doi.org/10.7249/RR2273.

"Secretary Antony J. Blinken with Jake Tapper of State of the Union on CNN." Press release, U.S. Department of State, 15 August 2021.

"Security Council Endorses Afghanistan Agreement on Interim Arrangements Signed Yesterday in Bonn, Unanimously Adopting Resolution 1383." Press release, United Nations Security Council, 12 June 2001.

Sedra, Mark, ed. *Confronting Afghanistan's Security Dilemma: Reforming the Security Sector*, Brief 28. Bonn, Germany: Bonn International Center for Conversion, 2003.

——. "Security Sector Reform and State Building in Afghanistan." In *Afghanistan: Transition under Threat*. Edited by Geoffrey Hayes and Mark Sedra. Waterloo, Canada: Wilfred Laurier University Press, 2008.

Self-Reliance through Mutual Accountability Framework (SMAF). Kabul: Islamic Republic of Afghanistan, 2015.

Shaikh, Saleem, and Sughra Tunio. "Pakistan Ramps Up Coal Power with Chinese-backed Plants." *Reuters*, 2 May 2017.

Shesgreen, Deirdre. "Trump's Ex-national Security Adviser H. R. McMaster Warns Afghan Peace Talks Will Fail, Leave US Vulnerable." *USA Today*, 21 September 2020.

Siddique, Abubakar. *Afghanistan's Ethnic Divides*. Oslo: Norwegian Peacebuilding Resource Centre, Norwegian Ministry of Foreign Affairs, 2012.

Silberman, James M., and Charles Weiss Jr. *Restructuring for Productivity: The Technical Assistance Program of the Marshall Plan as a Precedent for the Former Soviet Union*, Industry Series Paper No. 64. Washington, DC: World Bank, 1992.

Specia, Megan. " 'A Dumb Decision:' U.S. Said to Waste $28 Million on Afghan Army Camouflage." *New York Times*, 21 June 2017.

Straziuso, Jason. "Afghan High Court Extends Karzai's Term 3 Months." *Toronto (Canada) Star*, 29 March 2009.

Takala, Rudy. "John Bolton Blames Trump for Afghanistan: 'Negotiators Delegitimized the Afghan Government'." *Mediaite*, 27 August 2021.

"Taliban Religious Police Jail Beard-trimmers for 10 Days." RAWA News, 18 December 1999.

"Taliban Takeover of Afghanistan Is an 'American Catastrophe,' H. R. McMaster Says." PBS News Hour, 16 August 2021.

"Taliban Territory: Life in Afghanistan under the Militants." BBC News, 8 June 2017.

Tanzeem, Ayesha. "Afghans Fear Taliban Return to Power after Withdrawal of US Forces." *VOA News*, 4 May 2021.

Tarnoff, Curt. *The Marshall Plan: Design, Accomplishments, and Significance*. Washington, DC: Congressional Research Service, 2018.

Tellis, Ashley J. *Reconciling with the Taliban?: Toward an Alternative*

Grand Strategy in Afghanistan. Washington, DC: Carnegie Endowment for International Peace, 2009.

"Terror Attacks Hit U.S." CNN, 11 September 2001.

Thackery, Miss. *Mrs. Dymond*, vol. 1. Leipzig, Germany: Bernhard Tauchnitz, 1886.

The 2009 Presidential and Provincial Council Elections. Washington, DC: National Democratic Institute, 2010.

The 9/11 Commission Report: Final Report of the National Commission on Terrorist Attacks upon the United States. Washington, DC: National Commission on Terrorist Attacks upon the United States, 2004.

The Budget and Expenditures for the Development of Economic Analysis. Kabul: Ministry of Finance, Islamic Republic of Afghanistan, 2020.

The Cost of War: Afghan Experiences of Conflict, 1978–2009. Kabul: Afghanistan Civil Society Forum, 2009.

The Department of State Bulletin, vol. 28, 14 January 1952.

The Department of State Bulletin, vol. 82, June 1982.

The Global War on Terrorism: The First 100 Days. Washington, DC: White House, 2001.

"The IMF at a Glance." International Monetary Fund, 3 March 2021.

"The London Conference and the Afghanistan Compact." Department of State, 31 January 2006.

The Marshall Plan: Lessons Learned for the 21st Century. Paris: OECD Publishing, 2008. https://doi.org/10.1787/978 9264044258-en.

The Papers of George Catlett Marshall, vol. 6, *"The Whole World Hangs in the Balance," January 8, 1947–September 30, 1949*. Baltimore, MD: Johns Hopkins University Press, 2013.

The State of Food and Agriculture, 1955: Review of a Decade and Outlook. Rome, Italy: Food and Agriculture Organization, United Nations, 1955.

The State of the World's Children 2019: Children, Food, and Nutrition—Growing Well in a Changing World. New York: UNICEF, 2019.

"The U.S. War in Afghanistan 1999–2021." Council on Foreign Relations, accessed 12 July 2021.

Todaro, Michael P., and Stephen C. Smith. *Economic Development*, 8th ed. Harlow, UK: Pearson, 2003.

"Tokyo Mutual Accountability Framework." USAID, 8 July 2012.

Trump, Donald J. "Remarks by President Trump on the Strategy in Afghanistan and South Asia." Speech, Fort Myer, Arlington, VA, 21 August 2017.

Turton, David, and Peter Marsden. *Taking Refugees for a Ride?: The Politics of Refugee Return*, Issues Paper Series. Kabul: Afghanistan Research and Evaluation Unit, 2002.

"Two Million Children under Five Suffering from Acute Malnutrition in Afghanistan." Press release, UNICEF, accessed 10 September 2021.

"Unemployment Rate Spikes in Afghanistan." *TOLO News*, 2 October 2015.

"United Arab Emirates Won't Recognize Taliban." ABC News, 7 January 2006.

"UN to Present Plans for Rebuilding Afghanistan at Donor Conference in Tokyo." *UN News*, 18 January 2002.

U.S. Congress, House of Representatives, Committee on Appropriations, Subcommittee on Foreign Operations, Export Financing, and Related Programs, USAID Accomplishments in Afghanistan. 109th Cong., 1st Sess. (11 September 2006).

"US Rocked by Terror Attacks." BBC News, 11 September 2001.

"US Says Drone Kills Suicide Bombers Targeting Kabul Airport." *Al Jazeera*, 29 August 2021.

Waldman, Matt. *Falling Short: Aid Effectiveness in Afghanistan*, ACBAR Advocacy Series. Kabul, Afghanistan: Oxfam International, 2008.

Walsh, Mary. "11 Days in August: How Afghanistan Fell." CBS News, 22 August 2021.

Ward, Clarissa, Tim Lister, Angela Dewan, and Saleem Mehsud. "Afghan President Ashraf Ghani Flees the Country as Taliban Forces Enter the Capital." CNN, 16 August 2021.

Wellman, Phillip Walter. "White House: Afghanistan Opium Yield Expected to Rise Even as Acreage Planted to Poppies Falls." *Stars and Stripes*, 10 February 2020.

Welna, David. "In Reversal, Afghan Leader Agrees to Release Taliban Prisoners." NPR, 11 March 2020.

"Whistleblower Exposed Fraud by the Louis Berger Group; $69.3 Million Settlement Sets Record for Afghanistan and Iraq Contractor Fraud Case." Cision PR Newswire, 5 November 2010.

"Who Is Osama Bin Laden?." BBC News, 18 September 2001.

Wilder, Andrew. *Cops or Robbers?: The Struggle to Reform the Afghan National Police*, Issues Paper Series. Kabul: Afghanistan Research and Evaluation Unit, 2007.

Williams, Warren. "Flashpoint Austria: The Communist-Inspired Strikes of 1950." *Journal of Cold War Studies* 9, no. 3 (2007).

Wilson, Scott, and Jon Cohen. "Poll: Nearly Two-thirds of Americans Say Afghan War Isn't Worth Fighting." *Washington Post*, 15 March 2011.

"World Bank Funds Transferred to the Government of the Islamic Republic of Afghanistan to Fight COVID-19 Pandemic." Press release, World Bank, 20 April 2020.

"World Development Indicators." World Bank, accessed 9 July 2021.

Wright, Donald P. *A Different Kind of War: The United States Army in Operation Enduring Freedom.* Fort Leavenworth, KS: Combat Studies Institute Press, U.S. Army Combined Arms Center, 2010.

Wu, Z. *Afghanistan: Andkhoy-Qaisar Road Project*, Completion Report No. 37075. Mandaluyong, Philippines: Asian Development Bank, 2010.

Zarr, Gerald. "The Marshall Plan: Rebuilding a Devastated Europe." *History Magazine*, October/November 2012.

Zink, Harold. *The United States in Germany, 1944–1955.* Princeton, NJ: D. Van Nostrand 1957.

INDEX

223

ABOUT THE AUTHOR

Abid Amiri is an Afghan American currently working as an economist in Washington, DC. He was the policy director for the Ministry of Finance in Afghanistan between 2016 and 2018. Prior to joining the Policy Department, he was an economic advisor to the Minister of Finance, Eklil Hakimi. Amiri has a wide range of domestic and international work experience in the development sector. He worked as the economic affairs officer for the Embassy of Afghanistan in Washington between 2012 and 2014. Moreover, he has worked for a number of nonprofit organizations based in Washington and Afghanistan.

Amiri holds a master's degree in international development studies from George Washington University in Washington and a bachelor's degree in economics and global studies from St. Lawrence University in New York. He has a number of publications including his work on *Road Reconstruction in Post-Conflict Afghanistan: A Cure or a Curse?* (2013) and a 2010 article on unemployment in Afghanistan in the *Global Journal*. Amiri is fluent in Pashto, Dari, and English.